LET'S EAT
French

Jean Conil

Editor
Barbara Croxford

truefoulsham
LONDON • NEW YORK • TORONTO • SYDNEY

foulsham

Yeovil Road, Slough, Berkshire, SL1 4JH

ISBN 0-572-01834-7

Copyright © 1993 Strathearn Publishing Ltd.

All rights reserved.

The Copyright Act (1956) prohibits (subject to certain very limited exceptions) the making of copies of any copyright work or of a substantial part of such a work, including the making of copies by photocopying or similar process. Written permission to make a copy or copies must therefore normally be obtained from the publisher in advance. It is advisable also to consult the publisher if in any doubt as to the legality of any copying which is to be undertaken.

Photoset in Great Britain by Encounter Photosetting, Fleet, Hampshire
Printed in Great Britain by Cox & Wyman Ltd, Reading, Berkshire

Contents

Introduction

French cooking is not as complex as people imagine. It is in fact very simple. Most main dishes are usually accompanied by one vegetable only, often potatoes or pasta. Specific vegetable dishes and salads are served as a course.

In 'Let's Eat French' I have concentrated on dishes which have been accepted abroad as more popular and can be identified just by their names such as Soupe à l'oignon, Boeuf Bourguignon, Carré d'agneau, Pommes Lyonnaise, Petits pois à la Française, Sole bonne femme, Coquille St Jacques, Moules marinières, Crème caramel, Poire Belle Hélène.

The preparation of these recipes varies in time, depending on the main ingredient. Moules marinières only takes 5 minutes, but a beef Bourguignon will take 2-3 hours to prepare and cook. Time is money in French cooking and 'Waste Not, Want Not' is our motto.

In all areas of culinary craftsmanship, there is a method and techniques to make the work easier. Advanced preparation will help you cut corners in all directions, as well as a well equipped kitchen which will make the cooking more interesting. So let us review the ideal set-up in your own home:

The Kitchen
Area size 3.5 x 3.5 metres/14 x 14 ft, large enough to hold a

cooker, table, six chairs, fridge/freezer, microwave, cupboards, working space, one double sink, with a large window overlooking the garden of your house, if possible. A good ventilation system provided by a canopy over your cooker is ideal.

Equipment and Tools
One whisk, one moulinette, one blender, one set of six knives, one rolling pin and pastry board, one pair of good scales, measuring jugs, baking and roasting trays, one set of heavy based pans, omelette and pancake pans, one thermometer, one sugar thermometer.

Cupboard Space
For all your dry groceries to include assorted spices and dry herbs, flour, sugar, and also items like meat extracts, oil and vinegar.

A well aerated space for your fresh vegetables and fruits.

One bottle rack for your wines.

Advanced preparations for cooking

●   Compile menus for the whole week. List your ingredients accordingly.

●   Read the recipe and prepare all ingredients – cleaning, washing, draining and arrange them in small cups or containers.

●   Prepare garnishes and sauces in advance of the main dish where possible.

●   Short time dishes can be prepared 15 minutes before the meal. Longer cooking can often be done the day before. A Boeuf Bourguignon will reheat well.

●   Have fresh herbs and green leaves to flavour or garnish your main dishes.

● Economy plays an important part in French cooking. Work out the cost according to what you can afford. Prepare a weekly budget and stick to it. The best dishes are often the cheapest.

Kitchen Knowledge

The principles of French gastronomy are based on nutritional factors as well as taste and flavour. In LET'S EAT FRENCH, the dishes have been composed with balanced diets in mind.

Shopping Hints

Buy home produced food in the season. For example, chicken and meats are good all the year round at a steady price, whereas local strawberries are best bought in June than imported from Africa in December. The modern shopper should not be too fussy in selecting the right ingredient, as what is available in any supermarket should reflect a good bargain in relation to quality and price.

Diet

The bulk of your shopping must be fresh vegetables and fruits, in the ratio of 3 to 1 with protein foods – dairy products, fish, poultry and meat. This means for every 1.5 kg/3 lb weight of vegetables and fruits, you match it with a total of 450 g/1 lb of a mixture of eggs milk, cheese, fish, poultry and meat. Remembering that you can find good protein substitutes in cereals (bread, corn, barley) and legumes (peas, beans, léntils) etc.

To make it simpler, here is an average diet for one person: 600 ml/1 pint/2½ cups fresh milk, 50 g/2 oz low fat cheese, 1 egg, 100 g/4 oz meat, poultry or fish, 50 g/2 oz/ ¼ cup butter or vegetable margarine or unsaturated oil, 250 g/8 oz root vegetables or peas or beans, 250 g/8 oz fresh fruits or green vegetables or salad leaves. This would give you an average of 60-70 g/2½ oz of protein with a total 2500 calories.

Varieties of food and styles of preparations are the main elements of French meals. Eat as much raw vegetables and fruits as possible by way of crudités in the form of starters or salads, or with cheese. Portion your food carefully to avoid left-overs. Reheated meat, fish or poultry never tastes as good as when cooked fresh.

Culinary Preparation

Plan your advance preparations. Wash, clean and trim your vegetables and arrange the cut ingredients in separate saucers or containers at your leisure.

Use the sauté pan or wok as much as possible for quick cooking for either poaching, sautéing or stir-frying.

- All root vegetables should be peeled, washed and cut in the size indicated in the recipe.

- All leaves should be washed in plenty of cold water, well drained and dried, with inedible stems and cores removed.

- All dried pulses and legumes are best soaked in distilled water rather than hard water for quicker tenderization.

- All non-starchy vegetables should be undercooked.

- Remove fat and bones from all fish, meat or poultry prior to cooking, this saves times.

- Use bones for stocks and gravies.

Flavouring

Use fresh herbs and spices whenever possible, and at the last moment, as the essential oils will evaporate in long cooking process or exposure to air resulting in lost aromatic flavours.

Fresh parsley should be washed and well drained before cutting or chopping.

Use herbs to enhance vegetables – caraway seeds with cabbage; sage and thyme with pork and ham; tarragon with poultry and fish; dill and horseradish with oily fish; chives with potatoes; basil with fish or vegetable soups; garlic with tomatoes or peppers; onions and mustard seeds with beef; cloves and cinnamon with salted and smoked meats.

Chef's Tips

- Shop around for the best bargains. Cut portions are not always the best buy.

- Make use of every part of meats – bones for stocks and gravies.

- Soft fruits can be made into purées or jams.

- Stale hard cheese should be grated or melted for fondues and rarebits or pasta dishes.

- Stale bread should be crumbled as a coating for deep fry dishes, or soup croûtons.

Presentation of Dishes

Whatever you think of Nouvelle Cuisine, it has its merit even in your home to make the food attractive, to catch the eye and tickle the palate. A lovely presentation will always be remembered by your guests and family. Learn to cut vegetables into flowers, use fresh leaves and berries to garnish your meat and poultry dishes. Cut your vegetables in fancy shapes geometrically. Success on the plate depends on the freshness of ingredients and last minute cooking attention.

Pay attention to nutritive factors. A well balanced menu demands knowledge of food health properties. Good food is nourishing food. Correct seasoning is also important not too salty, spicy or sweet. Enjoy your meals with Let's Eat French. Bon Appetit!

Jean Conil

Soups

General Notes

I have grouped soups and sauces next to each other because they can easily be converted into each other, onion sauce into onion soup, mushroom sauce to mushroom soup, tomato sauce to tomato soup and so on. Speed of preparation is essential in getting results quickly, hence my recommendation for using the blender. In an instant, you can make a soup or a sauce just before a meal.

Some soups and sauces can be enriched with purée of fish and shellfish as in Bisque de Crevettes, with cream and egg yolks, others with cheese as in Soupe à l'Oignon Gratinée.

The garnishing of soups with bread sippets, croûtons, cheese sticks, as well as additional solid meat ingredients, can help in making the soup a meal in itself.

For busy housewives, cutting corners in cooking is a bonus. One can use packet soups for convenience, fresh soups can be made by using stock cubes and meat or vegetable extracts to save time in stock-making.

Most purée soups can be made by using left-over vegetables. The best thickener for vegetable soup is made with potatoes added to other ingredients as a Crème Vichyssoise or Potage St Germain. But the use of cornflour (cornstarch), sago, semolina, rice or vermicelli and other pasta is also the means of building up a simple vegetable soup into a grand potage.

For quick sauces, the use of beef gravy or chicken granules is much welcomed, particularly to accompany steaks and grills. The addition of a little wine in the pan with the meat juices will provide a flavouring element and the granules the thickening finish.

The lingering aroma of herbs and spices added at the very last minute to soups and sauces provides the final touch; such herbs, as thyme with brown soups and sauces, tarragon and basil with fish soups and sauces, parsley, garlic, dill, chives, or spices such as cinnamon, cloves, nutmeg and mace, will be useful all the time.

SOUPE A L'OIGNON GRATINEE

Onion and cheese soup

Ingredients

1 large onion
15 ml/1 tbsp cooking oil
45 ml/3 tbsp butter
22.5 ml/1½ tbsp plain (all-purpose) flour
5 ml/1 tsp sugar
1 litre/1¾ pints/4¼ cups water
100 ml/4 fl oz/½ cup fortified wine – white port or dry Madeira
10 ml/2 tsp salt
6 ml/1¼ tsp black pepper
6 slices of French bread, toasted
100 g/4 oz/ 1 cup hard cheese – Cheddar, Gruyère or Emmenthal, grated

Method

1. Cut the onion in half and slice thinly.

2. Heat the oil and butter in a thick based pan and sizzle the onion until translucent and pale in colour. Add the flour and sugar, stirring for a few seconds.

3. Gradually stir in the water. Bring to the boil and keep bubbling for 12 minutes. Blend your favourite wine into the soup. Season to taste.

4. Pour the soup into individual flameproof soup terrines (250 ml/8 fl oz/1 cup capacity). Top with a slice of toasted bread and sprinkle with grated cheese.

5. Brown the soup under the grill (broiler) to melt the cheese. Serve piping hot.

Serves 6

2 POTAGE ST GERMAIN

Pea soup

Ingredients

450 g/1 lb mangetout peas (snow peas)
225 g/8 oz potatoes, peeled
45 ml/3 tbsp butter
1 medium onion, chopped
600 ml/1 pint/2½ cups water or stock
300 ml/½ pint/1¼ cups milk or single (light) cream
Salt and pepper
Grated nutmeg
5 ml/1 tsp sugar

Method

1. Top and tail the peas. Cut the potatoes and peas into small pieces.

2. Heat the butter in a large 2.25 litre/4 pint/5 pint saucepan and stir fry the onion for a few seconds, then add the peas and potatoes and cover with water. Boil for 12 minutes until the potatoes are soft.

3. Blend to a purée. Reheat with the milk or cream. Season with salt, pepper, grated nutmeg and sugar. Serve with fried croûtons or sippets of bread.

    Note: Ordinary frozen or dried peas can also be used. (Dried peas need soaking.)

Serves 6

3 SOUPE ESAU

Lentil soup

Ingredients

45 ml/3 tbsp vegetable oil
1 large onion, diced
1 medium carrot, chopped
225 g/8 oz/1 cup green lentils
1.5 litres/2½ pints/6¼ cups water
2 beef stock cubes
Salt and pepper
Ground mace
15 ml/1 tbsp tomato purée
15 ml/1 tbsp cornflour (cornstarch) blended with
75 ml/5 tbsp water

Method

1. Heat the oil in a large saucepan and stir fry the onion and carrot for 5 minutes. Add the lentils and water and boil for 20 minutes.

2. Add the stock cubes and check the seasoning before adding salt, then pepper and ground mace. Blend in the tomato purée and reboil.

3. Stir the blended cornflour into the soup. Boil for 4 minutes more to a creamy consistency. Rub the soup through a sieve or purée in a blender. Reheat before serving with fried croûtons.

   Variation: Add either milk or cream to make the soup smoother.

Serves 6

CREME VICHYSSOISE

Potato and leek soup

Ingredients

60 ml/4 tbsp butter and oil, mixed
1 leek, sliced thinly, washed and drained
225 g/8 oz potatoes, peeled and diced
1.5 litres/2½ pints/6¼ cups water
150 ml/¼ pint/⅔ cup single (light) cream or milk
Salt and pepper
Grated nutmeg
45 ml/3 tbsp chives

Method

1. Heat the butter and oil in a large saucepan and stir fry the vegetables for 5 minutes to develop flavour without browning. Add the water and simmer for 15 minutes. Pass through a sieve or purée in a blender.

2. Reheat the soup with the cream or milk. Season to taste with salt, pepper and grated nutmeg. Add the chopped chives to serve.

   Variations: For a cold soup, blend in a cupful of single or sour cream and serve icy cold.

   A few leaves of watercress would add piquancy to the soup.

Serves 6

5 SOUPE PROVENÇALE AU PISTOU

Vegetable soup with basil

The secret of this soup is in the flavouring of garlic and basil.

Ingredients

150 g/5 oz potatoes, peeled and cut into strips
1 medium carrot
1 leek, washed
1.5 litres/2½ pints/6¼ cups water

For the pistou paste:
3 cloves of garlic
6 skinned almonds
30 ml/2 tbsp tomato purée
6 basil leaves or 5 ml/1 tsp dried basil
45 ml/3 tbsp olive oil
Salt and pepper to taste

Method

1. Thinly slice the vegetables about 0.5 cm/¼ inch thick and place in a large saucepan. Cover with the water, bring to the boil and simmer for 15 minutes until tender.

2. Blend or pound the Pistou ingredients to a paste and dilute into the soup. Season to taste.

   Variation: If liked, the soup can be garnished with vermicelli. Simmer the vermicelli for 2 minutes in water. Drain and add to soup at the last moment.

Serves 6

6 BISQUE DE CREVETTES

Prawn soup

The characteristic flavour of a prawn bisque is obtained from the shell of the prawn rather than the flesh, so it is better to make this soup in two quick steps. This simplified method gives a very good result.

Ingredients

225 g/8 oz/1⅓ cups medium or large prawns (shrimp) in the shell, raw or cooked
300 ml/½ pint/1¼ cups water
45 ml/3 tbsp olive oil
1 small onion, chopped
1 small carrot, chopped
30 ml/2 tbsp flour
15 ml/1 tbsp tomato purée
60 ml/4 tbsp medium sherry
150 ml/¼ pint/⅔ cup single (light) cream
Salt and pepper

Method

1. Shell the prawns and boil the shells in the water for 5 minutes. Strain the liquid.

2. Heat the oil in a saucepan and stir fry the onion and carrot for 4 minutes. Add the flour, tomato purée and prawn liquid. Boil for 10 minutes, then blend to a purée.

3. Add the shelled prawns and sherry and boil for 5 minutes. Lastly blend in the cream and season to taste. (The texture of the soup can be adjusted by the addition of a little milk or extra cream.)

Serves 4

Sauces

General Notes

The modern practice of producing French sauces has changed considerably over the past decades. Many famous chefs are now using stock cubes and meat glaze concentrates, and even prepared powder sauces. All that is required to make this basic convenience sauce alive with good flavours is herbs, spices and wine. The fish, meat or poultry will impart their own flavours, thus improving the sauces even more.

From one basic brown and white sauce, many variations can be made to suit many dishes.

BASIC BROWN SAUCE

This is a basic brown sauce suitable for all red meats.

Ingredients

30 ml/2 tbsp vegetable oil
1 medium onion, chopped
1 medium carrot, chopped
1 stalk of celery, sliced
15 ml/1 tbsp flour
15 ml/1 tbsp tomato purée
600 ml/1 pint/2½ cups water
2 beef stock cubes or 15 ml/1 tbsp marmite
1 sprig of thyme
1 clove of garlic
Salt and pepper

Method

1. In a heavy based saucepan, capacity 1.2 litres/ 2 pints/5 cups, heat the oil and stir fry the vegetables until pale brown. Add the flour and tomato purée and cook for 30 seconds.

2. Blend the water into this mixture with the rest of the ingredients, except the seasoning. Boil for 15 minutes, then strain. Season to taste.

Brown Sauce Variations

Sauce Chasseur Heat 15 ml/1 tbsp oil in a shallow pan and sauté 1 small chopped shallot and 4 sliced mushrooms for 1 minute. Add 1 small glass of red or white wine and a pinch of tarragon. Boil for 2 minutes, then blend in 300 ml/½ pint/1¼ cups of the Brown Sauce. This sauce is ideal for steaks and fried chicken pieces.

Sauce Provençale Heat 30 ml/2 tbsp olive oil and shallow fry 3 cloves of garlic for 30 seconds. Add 4 tomatoes, skinned, seeded and chopped, 1 small sachet of saffron or 4 basil leaves. Cook for 4 minutes, then add 300 ml/½ pint/1¼ cups of the Brown Sauce. Boil for 2 minutes and strain. Use this sauce for pasta, chicken dishes and veal cutlets.

Sauce Bordelaise Heat 30 ml/2 tbsp butter and oil in a pan and stir fry 2 chopped shallots for 1 minute. Pour in 1 large glass of red wine and boil for 3 minutes. Blend in 300 ml/½ pint/1¼ cups of the Brown Sauce. Reboil and strain. Use for steaks, chicken or oily fish like salmon.

Makes 600 ml/1 pint/2½ cups

2 | BASIC WHITE SAUCE

This basic white sauce, known as Béchamel, can be used for fish, white meats and poultry and for white vegetables such as onions, cauliflower, white chicory, turnips or mushrooms.

Ingredients

600 ml/1 pint/2½ cups milk
1 small onion, studded with 2 cloves
45 ml/3 tbsp butter or vegetable margarine
45 ml/3 tbsp plain (all-purpose) flour
Salt and pepper

Method

1. Bring the milk to the boil with the onion and simmer for 5 minutes. Remove from the heat and take out the onion.

2. In a smaller saucepan, melt the butter or margarine and add the flour. Cook for 1 minute, without browning. Gradually add the milk and stir to avoid lumps. Season to taste. (Strain the sauce if lumpy.)

White Sauce Variations

Mornay sauce Add 50 g/2 oz/½ cup grated hard cheese to 600 ml/1 pint/2½ cups White Sauce. For further enrichment, 45 ml/3 tbsp double (heavy) cream can be added to the sauce. For a gratin sauce, add 2 egg yolks to the sauce and reheat until boiling point.

Sauce vin blanc To the basic White Sauce, add 75 ml/3 fl oz/⅓ cup fish liquor, in which the fish has been cooked in dry white wine, and juice of ½ lemon.

Sauce aux herbes To the basic White Sauce, add 30 ml/2 tbsp chopped fresh parsley and tarragon.

Sauce aux champignons Boil 1 chopped shallot in 1 glass of dry white wine with 50 g/2 oz/½ cup sliced white mushrooms and a pinch of tarragon. Add this to the basic White Sauce without straining.

Makes 600 ml/1 pint/2½ cups

3   MAYONNAISE

Ingredients

5 ml/1 tsp made Dijon mustard
3 egg yolks
Salt and pepper
300 ml/½ pint/1¼ cups olive oil
5 ml/1 tsp hot wine vinegar

Method

1. In a bowl place the made mustard, egg yolks, and salt and pepper. 5 ml/1 tsp salt is enough and a good pinch of white pepper.

2. Gradually whisk the mixture. Very gently let the oil drip in as you whisk. The mixture will emulsify and thicken providing the oil is added in a steady stream. When very thick, add the hot vinegar.

Hors d'oeuvre dips

Tomato Dip Pass two hard-boiled eggs through a sieve to obtain a paste. Blend in 300 ml/½ pint/ 1¼ cups Mayonnaise, 30 ml/2 tbsp of tomato ketchup and 15 ml/1 tbsp Worcestershire sauce.

Herb Dip Blend 100 g/4 oz/½ cup cream cheese into 300 ml/½ pint/1¼ cups Mayonnaise. Flavour with a mixture fresh chopped herbs – parsley, basil and mint. Alternatively, use pickled gherkins.

Mushroom Dip Cook 100 g/4 oz/1 cup chopped mushrooms in a pan with 15 ml/1 tbsp oil for 3 minutes. Cool, then add 300 ml/½ pint/1¼ cups Mayonnaise.

Aubergine Dip Peel and slice 1 aubergine (egg-plant). Fry the slices in 60 ml/4 tbsp olive oil. Blend the mixture with 1 chopped shallot. Cool and blend in 600 ml/1 pint/2½ cups Mayonnaise.

Humus Dip Blend 100 g/4 oz cooked chickpea purée (garbanzo beans) with 300 ml/½ pint/1¼ cups Mayonnaise. Flavour the dip with chopped chives.

Cocktail sauces

To change these dips into tasty prawn or fish cocktail sauces:

● Thin down Tomato Dip with 30 ml/2 tbsp tomato juice.

● Thin down Mushroom Dip with 30 ml/2 tbsp mushroom ketchup or HP fruit sauce.

● Thin down any of the above dips with 15 ml/ 1 tbsp anchovy sauce with 45 ml/ 3 tbsp hot White Sauce (page 22).

Makes about 300 ml/½ pint/1¼ cups

Chef's tips

- Better stocks are made with boiled shin of beef, veal or gammon.

- To degrease sauces, apply a piece of greaseproof (wax) paper or tissue to the surface of the sauce. The fat floating on top will be removed.

- To transform a sauce into a soup, add a purée of vegetables, such as peas, beans, potatoes, tomatoes, carrots, onions etc in the ratio of 100 ml/4 fl oz/ ½ cup purée per 600 ml/1 pint/2½ cups sauce.

- To improve the wine flavour in sauces, use fortified wines such as vermouth, sherry, white port, Madeira or even brandy can strengthen the sauce. Alcohol retains flavour but loses its pungency when the sauce is boiled. Use ten per cent or 60 ml/2 fl oz/¼ cup per 600 ml/1 pint/2½ cups white sauce or 1 small glass.

- To improve a brown sauce for steaks, use coarsely ground black pepper or green peppercorns. A little chopped chilli will also give a lift to the sauce.

- Diluted made mustard added to white sauce will be suitable for grilled fish. The sauce must not boil after the addition of mustard. The ratio of made mustard for mustard sauce is 15 ml/1 tbsp per 600 ml/1 pint/2½ cups white sauce.

- Sour cream or yoghurt can improve acidity for fish sauces but it must not boil after it has been added.The ratio of sour cream or yoghurt is 75 ml/3 fl oz/⅓ cup per 600 ml/1 pint/2½ cups white sauce.

- For a more fishy taste to white sauce used for fish, add Taramasalata, made with smoked cod's roe. Use 30 ml/2 tbsp taramasalata per 600 ml/ 1 pint/2½ cups white sauce.

- For marinades and barbecue sauces, see Meat on page 60. Or use convenience bottled sauces, such as Worcestershire.

COGNAC

Eggs

General Notes

Whether you buy free range or battery, eggs must be very
fresh. One way to make sure is to break one on a saucer, if it
is very fresh the egg white should be firm and gluey, if it is
watery or runny, the egg is stale.

As well as a breakfast, egg dishes are much appreciated
for lunch or high tea. What is more delicious than a light
omelette with a salad and a glass of red wine? Scrambled
eggs can be served hot with cold smoked salmon. Hard-
boiled eggs are excellent as a garnish for salads.

In different recipes which require either egg yolks or the
whites; for meringue for instance, the unused egg yoiks
should be used up in making pastry dough or pasta dough
or in creamed potatoes. Never waste them.

NOUILLES AUX LEGUMES

Stir fried egg noodles with vegetable strips

Ingredients

450 g/1 lb vegetables, such as French beans, celery,
carrots, turnips, bean shoots, mushroom, onions, fennel,
bean sprouts
Salt and pepper
225 g/8 oz egg noodles, cooked
5 ml/1 tsp anis powder
105 ml/7 tbsp oil
Chinese or Cos lettuce leaves to serve

Method

1. Prepare all the vegetables and cut into thin julienne
   strips. Add seasoning.

2. Boil the egg noodles for 5 minutes, then drain.

3. Heat the oil in a wok or large shallow pan and stir
   fry the vegetables for 3 minutes. Add the cooked
   noodles and stir fry for 1 minute more. Season and
   add anis powder. Serve on plates lined with
   Chineses or Cos lettuce leaves.

Wines

Rosé or Cabernet Sauvignon

Serves 6

2 OMELETTE SOUFFLEE AUX ASPERGES

Asparagus soufflé omelette

The secret of this feather-light omelette is in making a meringue of the egg whites and blending the egg yolks separately. It can be stuffed with savoury or sweet ingredients – cheese, herbs, mushrooms or fruits.

Ingredients

3 large fresh eggs, separated, size 1 or 2
Salt and pepper
30 ml/2 tbsp butter
15 ml/1 tbsp oil
4 asparagus tips, cooked and cut in small pieces

Method

1. In a clean fat-free mixing bowl, place the egg whites. Using a balloon or coil whisk, beat the egg whites until it holds in the whisk. Gently fold in the egg yolks and season to taste.

2. Heat the butter and oil in a small frying pan or omelette pan. Pour the egg mixture into the foaming butter. Cook for 2 minutes over a very low heat. With a palette knife, lift the omelette to make sure the bottom part does not get too brown.

3. Fill with the asparagus pieces. Fold the omelette in two and slip it onto a flat ovenproof serving dish. Bake in a preheated oven at 200°C/400°F/gas mark 6 for 4 minutes to allow it to puff up. Serve immediately.

Wines

Chablis, Sancerre, Muscadet or a red Claret.

Serves 1

3 OEUF EN COCOTTE A LA CREME

Egg poached in a ramekin

Eggs served in ramekin dishes should never be seasoned.

Ingredients

15 ml/1 tbsp butter
45 ml/3 tbsp double (heavy) cream
1-2 eggs

Method

1. Butter a 200 ml/⅓ pint/1 cup capacity ramekin dish. Pour in the cream and break in one or two eggs. Place the ramekin dish in a shallow tray half filled with water, on top of the stove.

2. Cover the ramekin dish with foil. Bring the water to the boil and cook for 8 minutes. When the white is set, the egg is ready. (Leave any seasoning to the person eating the egg.)

Serves 1

4 TORTE AUX BLETTES

Swiss chard tart

The leaves of this vegetable with firm white stems and green leaves is an excellent vegetable and a filling for this tart, a speciality of my own country town of Amiens. Also known as seakale beet.

Ingredients

450 g/1 lb prepared puff pastry

For the filling:
45 ml/3 tbsp butter
450 g/1 lb Swiss chard leaves
1 medium onion, chopped

For the sauce:
150 ml/¼ pint/⅔ cup White Sauce (page 22)
3 eggs, beaten
Salt and pepper
Grated nutmeg
1 egg yolk for glazing

Method

1. Wash the chard and drain well. Cut into shreds.

2. Heat the butter in a large pan and stir fry the chard leaves and onion for 4 minutes until cooked. Remove from the heat. Drain the mixture, pressing to eliminate the juices.

3. Blend 2 beaten eggs into the cold white sauce and add the cooked chard leaves. Season with salt, pepper and nutmeg.

4. Oil well a metal tart tin, 20 cm/8 inches in diameter.

5.　Divide the puff pastry in half. Roll each one to a 23cm/9 inch round. Line the tin with one round of pastry. Prick the bottom with a fork and rest for 10 minutes. Bake in a preheated oven at 200°C/400°F/gas mark 6 for 25 minutes. Cool.

6.　When cold, fill with the chard mixture. Cover with the other round of pastry. Seal the edges and make criss-cross lines on top. Brush with egg yolk and bake at the same temperature for another 12-15 minutes until golden. Serve hot or cold.

Wines

Light dry rosé, Graves or dry cider.

Serves 6

Seafood Selection

General Notes

There was a time not so long ago when fish was plentiful and cheap. Today with restriction on quotas of fish imposed by the EEC regulations, the fisherman is out of work and the fishmongers have to rely on expensive importation of odd fish one has never heard or dreamt of eating: shark steak, whale meat, swordfish are on the slab waiting to be sampled.

The firm favourites are still the flat fish varieties: sole, turbot, plaice and the round fish: salmon, trout, cod, haddock, and in the shell, scallops and mussels remain very popular.

Fried and grilled fish are still much preferred whether cooked in butter or in oil. The flavour is more distinctive. Poached fish dishes cooked in white wines are still in great demand – Sole Bonne Femme – although the same recipe can be used for any fish even with monkfish.Plaice tastes better fried or grilled as the flesh is soft. But fresh cod and haddock are best deep fried in batter or crumbs. Poach smoked fish in water or milk.

Prized salmon needs a simple method of cooking, poached in salted water and served hot with hollandaise or cold with mayonnaise; salmon is still the king of fish!

MOULES MARINIERES

Mussels in white wine

Because molluscs like mussels and scallops are cooked briefly, they must be absolutely fresh and are usually sold alive. Although cooked mussels are also available, the marinière preparation would not be suitable. All seaweeds attached to mussels should be removed and the mussels scraped and washed in salted water. Whatever the method, mussels only take 5 minutes to cook through. If overdone they tend to be tough and rubbery.

Ingredients

30 ml/2 tbsp butter
1 small onion, chopped
3 small shallots, chopped
2 litres/3½ pints/4½ pints fresh mussels in the shell, cleaned
300 ml/½ pint/1¼ cups white wine, very dry
150 ml/¼ pint/⅔ cup water
1 sprig of thyme
Juice of 1 lemon or 7.5 ml/½ tbsp wine vinegar
15 ml/1 tbsp butter and 15 ml/1 tbsp flour creamed together
Salt and pepper
60 ml/4 tbsp chopped fresh parsley

Method

1. In a thick based pan, heat the butter and stir fry the onion and shallots without colouring for 1 minute. Add the mussels and cover with wine, water, thyme, lemon juice or vinegar. Boil for 5 minutes. Drain, collecting the cooking liquor through a colander placed over a bowl.

2. Quickly boil down the liquor in a saucepan for about 5 minutes to reduce it by half. Whisk in the butter paste to thicken the sauce. Season to taste with salt and black pepper. Reheat the mussels for 1 minute and sprinkle with parsley. Serve in soup plates, providing a container placed in the middle of the table for the shells.

Variations
Moules Normande: Add 120 ml/4 fl oz/½ cup cream.
Moules Provençale: Add chopped tomato pulp with basil and garlic.

Wines

The same wine as for cooking – Muscadet, Dry Graves, Chablis.

Serves 4

2 | LANGOUSTINES AU GRATIN

Dublin Bay prawns or scampi with cheese

This is the seawater variety of Nephros norvegicus not to be confused with freshwater crayfish or ecrevisse. Both shellfish can be cooked in the same way. For years now we have been able to purchase the frozen shelled variety. Scampi is cooked in 2 minutes; overcooking will spoil them.

Ingredients

1 kg/2¼ lb shelled scampi or Dublin Bay prawns
60 ml/4 tbsp seasoned flour
45 ml/3 tbsp butter
30 ml/2 tbsp chopped shallots
8 white mushrooms, sliced
75 ml/3 fl oz/6 tbsp white wine
1 sprig of thyme
15 ml/1 tbsp tarragon
90 ml/6 tbsp White Sauce (page 22)
60 ml/4 tbsp double (heavy) cream
Salt and pepper
45 ml/3 tbsp grated cheese

Method

1.   Coat the scampi in seasoned flour and shake off the surplus. Using a colander to handle the scampi.

2.   Heat the butter in a shallow pan and stir the shallots and mushrooms for 30 seconds. Add the scampi and sauté for 2 minutes. Remove the

scampi and vegetables and keep in a dish while completing the sauce.

3. Add the white wine, thyme and tarragon and quickly boil for 4 minutes to reduce. Blend in the white sauce and cream, boil for 1 minute. Season, then strain.

4. Place the scampi in individual flameproof dishes. Cover with the sauce. Sprinkle with grated cheese and brown under the grill (broiler) for 1 minute. The timing is very important in this operation. Serve with rice pilaff or mashed potatoes.

Wines

Hock or Moselle are ideal partners.

Serves 4

3 COQUILLE ST JACQUES BRETONNE

Scallops fried in breadcrumbs

The flesh and red coral are the only edible part of the scallop. This popular mollusc can be prepared in numerous ways in wine and in creamy sauces. The following recipe has been handed down to me from a generation of my family who ran fish restaurants in various sea ports of France. In Britain, scallops are sold both in or out of the shells. Allow 4 scallops per portion.

Ingredients

16 medium scallops
100 g/4 oz/1 cup seasoned flour
30 ml/2 tbsp chopped shallots
30 ml/2 tbsp chopped fresh parsley
5 ml/1 tsp dried thyme
225 g/8 oz/1 cup dry breadcrumbs
2 eggs, beaten
Oil for shallow frying
90 ml/6 tbsp white wine
300 ml/½ pint/1¼ cups Mayonnaise (page 24)
Chilli powder
Salt

Method

1.   Wash and pat dry each scallop. Remove the red coral and set aside. Cut the white flesh in slices if large. Coat in seasoned flour.

2.   In a bowl, combine the chopped shallots, parsley, thyme and breadcrumbs.

3.   Dip each scallop in beaten egg, then coat in the crumb mixture.

4.   Heat the oil in a shallow pan to smoking point and fry the scallops for 1 minute. Drain on absorbent kitchen paper.

5.   Meanwhile, poach the red coral in the white wine for 1 minute. Drain, reserving the wine. Chop the corals finely, then blend into the mayonnaise, with the wine liquor. Liquidize the sauce to a thinner purée. Season with a little chilli and salt. Serve separately with the scallops.

A wedge of lemon and a tossed green salad make the best garnish or accompany with Pommes Frites (page 104).

Wines

Muscadet or Sancere.

Serves 4

4 ROUGET GRILLEE PROVENCALE

Grilled red mullet with olive dressing

Red mullet is one of the most tasty fish and also the most expensive because of its popular appeal to gourmets. The liver of the fish is also considered a delicacy, lightly fried in oil. It is more convenient to have the fish filleted by your fishmonger and quicker too. Keep the red skin on one of the fillets.

Ingredients

2 red mullet, 225 g/8 oz each, filleted
Salt and pepper
60 ml/4 tbsp oil
2 cloves of garlic, chopped
60 ml/4 tbsp cream cheese, seasoned
15 ml/1 tbsp olive oil
2 rye crispbreads
30 ml/2 tbsp grated cheese

For the dressing:
45 ml/3 tbsp olive oil
15 ml/1 tbsp wine vinegar
3 basil leaves, chopped
15 ml/1 tbsp small pickled capers
6 stuffed olives, chopped
Salt and pepper

Method

1. Wash, pat dry and season the four fillets. Stir the garlic into the oil; liquidize together if possible. Brush the fish with oil and grill (broil) for 1 minute on each side.

2. Whisk all the dressing ingredients in a bowl.

3. Beat the cream cheese with 15 ml/1 tbsp olive oil and spread on the two rye crispbreads. Sprinkle with grated cheese and brown under a grill (broiler).

4. To serve, pour a pool of the dressing on two plates. Sandwich the two fish fillets and top with the toasted crispbreads. Serve with a tomato salad, using the same dressing.

Wines

Corbières or Rosé.

Serves 2

5 | SOLE BONNE FEMME

Sole with mushrooms

Probably one of the best known sole dishes. Dover sole is the best of the flat fish variety with a firm flesh; however, lemon sole can be used.

Ingredients

> 1 kg/2¼ lb Dover sole, both skins removed and filleted
> Salt and white pepper
> Butter for greasing
> 50 g/2 oz/½ cup white mushrooms, sliced
> 2 shallots, chopped
> 100 ml/4 fl oz/½ cup dry white wine
> 100 ml/4 fl oz/½ cup water
> 1 small sprig of thyme
> ½ fish stock cube
> 30 ml/2 tbsp unsalted butter
> 10 ml/2 tsp flour
> Juice of ½ lemon
> 30 ml/2 tbsp chopped fresh parsley

Method

1. Flatten the sole fillets slightly to prevent them from curling during cooking, using a mallet or rolling pin. Season with salt and pepper. Place the fillets on a well buttered shallow earthenware dish. Sprinkle the sliced mushrooms over.

2. In a saucepan, boil the shallots, wine, water, thyme and fish stock cube for 5 minutes. Season with pepper only. Pour this stock over the fish. Cover the fish with a lid or well oiled paper.

3. Bake in a preheated oven at 200°C/400°F/gas mark 6 for 8-10 minutes. Strain the fish liquor into a saucepan.

4. Cream the butter and flour to a paste and dilute it in the fish sauce to make a creamy consistency. Check seasoning, add the lemon juice and pour the sauce over the fish. Sprinkle over the parsley. Glaze the fish under the grill (broiler) to obtain a brown skin. Serve with new boiled or creamed potatoes.

Wines

Macon, Chablis or Muscadet.

Serves 2

Meat

General Notes

When you examine the meat counter of a supermarket,
your first impression of seeing so many different cuts of
meat neatly portioned, weighed and costed, is one of relief
in not having to butcher your own meats, as the hard work
of preparation has been done for you.

It is deceiving for the untrained cook to select the right
piece for grilling steaks for instance. There is a difference in
cost and in tenderness. From the dietary angle, all meats
tough or tender have the same percentage of protein, so for
tenderness meat has to be cooked in different ways.

As a rule, the most tender parts of meat in beef are taken
from the loin and ribs. The tougher parts are from the
shoulder and front and back legs.

If you like underdone steaks, as the French do, you can
try cheaper steaks sold as skirt steaks from the belly of the
animal or even from the best part of the topside (top round).

The better type of steaks are from the fillet (filet
mignon), sirloin, ribs and rump.

For veal, the most tender parts are all along the ribs and loin and also the legs. Stew meat is usually taken from the collar and shin of the animal.

In lamb, the best parts also are from the loin and ribs as cutlets. The roasting parts are from the legs and shoulder, and the stewing part from the collar.

In pork the same applies, the loin and rib parts are the most tender, including the fillet (tenderloin). The roasting joints are from the shoulder and legs.

In salted and cured pork, the legs are sold as ham and gammon. Legs of pork cured separately are called ham. The side part cured in one piece with the legs are called gammon, whether cured or smoked.

All cured ham or gammon or loin should be desalted in cold water for at least 2 hours for better taste.

A section on marinades for barbecue sauces is included.

1 BOEUF BOURGUIGNON

Beef stew in wine with button mushrooms

The popularity of this dish is due to the wine used. You would be surprised to notice the difference when cooking with heavier wines; the higher in alcohol the better. During the cooking, the alcohol content evaporates after having enhanced the aromatic ingredients in the stew, such as thyme, garlic, onion and mushrooms. All kinds of stewing beef can be used for a Boeuf Bourguignon. The best cuts are topside and silverside for the simple reason that the meat is leaner and can be cut in perfect cubes.

Ingredients

1 kg/2¼ lb beef, from topside (round) or silverside, cut in 2.5 cm/1 inch cubes
45 ml/3 tbsp flour
60 ml/4 tbsp oil
300 ml/½ pint/1¼ cups red wine
300 ml/½ pint/1¼ cups water
1 sprig of thyme
15 ml/1 tbsp tomato purée
1 stalk of celery, diced
2 cloves of garlic, crushed

For the garnish:
30 ml/2 tbsp oil
4 rashers of streaky bacon (slices), rindless and cut in pieces

12 button onions
12 button mushrooms
Salt and pepper
Mixed spices to taste
Chopped fresh parsley

Method

1.   Rub the beef in flour and shake off the surplus.

2.   Heat the oil in a heavy casserole. Sauté the meat
        cubes for 8 minutes until brown. Add the wine,
        water, thyme, tomato purée, celery and garlic.
        Bring to the boil. Transfer to a preheated oven at
        180°C/350°F/gas mark 4 for 1½-2 hours. Check the
        tenderness of the meat.

3.   Lastly, heat the oil and stir fry the bacon for
        2 minutes. Add the button onions and cook for
        1 minute, then add the mushrooms and cook for
        another minute. Remove and drain into a colander.

4.   Discard the thyme from the casserole. Add the
        cooked garnish to the stew, season and simmer for
        15 minutes only. Sprinkle with chopped parsley
        and serve with new boiled potatoes or shell pasta.

        Variation: For stronger wine flavour, add a glass
        of port.

Wines

Beaujolais, Macon or Bouzy.

Dessert

Tarte aux Prunes.

Serves 4

2 BOEUF EN DAUBE

Braised beef

Traditionally, the daube consisted of a large piece of beef which was larded with pork fat strips. This is no longer necessary as the quality of braising beef has much improved, plus people are reluctant to eat fatty meats. This is why I suggest the omission of lard in this classic dish. The meat is cut in larger cubes than for Boeuf Bourguignon. Each piece weighing about 50 g/2 oz, as big as an egg.

Ingredients

1.5 kg/3 lb braising beef from topside (round), silverside or thick flank, cubed
1 medium onion, sliced
12 small onions
6 carrots, sliced
1 sprig of thyme
2 cloves of garlic, crushed
2.5 ml/½ tsp ground cinnamon and cloves
Salt and pepper
2 litres/3½ pints/4½ pints red wine, 13% volume
Rind of bacon with fat in one piece
45 ml/3 tbsp chopped fresh parsley

Method

1.   Place the meat in a large bowl with a layer of onions, carrots, thyme, garlic and all the seasonings. Cover with the wine. Place a lid on top and leave to marinate overnight in the refrigerator.

2.   Scald the rind of bacon. Place this rind at the bottom of a heavy casserole, preferably metal. Alternate the meat and vegetables in rows to fit the

casserole. Add the marinade and cover with a lid.

3. Braise in a preheated oven at 160°C/325°F/gas mark 3 for 4-5 hours. Sprinkle with parsley and serve with new boiled potatoes or pasta shells and broccoli.

Wines

Cahors, Red Graves or Corbières.

Dessert

Meringue nest filled with fruit.

Serves 6

3 CARBONNADE DE BOEUF FLAMANDE

Braised steaks in beer

The range of braising steak is varied – chuck steak, silverside, thick flank or topside (round). One of the best methods I have tried is to soak the beef in black stout beer overnight, adding a little malt vinegar. This is a popular dish in all the beer-drinking regions of northern and eastern France.

Ingredients

4 braising steaks, 225 g/8 oz each and 2 cm/¾ inch thick
300 ml/½ pint/1¼ cups black or brown stout ale or beer
15 ml/1 tbsp malt vinegar
1 large sprig of thyme
45 ml/3 tbsp flour
45 ml/3 tbsp oil for shallow frying
2 large onions, sliced
15 ml/1 tbsp dark honey
300 ml/½ pint/1¼ cups water
Salt and pepper
Ground mace

Method

1. In a large, deep earthenware dish, place the steaks and cover with the beer, vinegar and thyme. Cover with a lid and leave overnight in the refrigerator.

2. Drain the steaks in a colander and collect the marinade liquid in a bowl. Pat dry the steaks and coat in flour. Shake off the surplus.

3. Heat the oil in a frying pan and shallow fry the steaks until brown for 2 minutes on each side. Remove and transfer them to a casserole or shallow earthenware dish.

4. Stir fry the onions for 2 minutes. Place them under the steaks. In the same pan, boil the beer marinade with the dark honey for 1 minute. Cover the steaks with this liquid, then add the water, salt, pepper and mace.

5. Place a lid on top of the dish. Braise in a preheated oven at 180°C/350°F/gas mark 4 for 1½-2 hours. Check the steaks after 1 hour and turn them over. Serve with sauté potatoes, French beans or braised chicory.

Drinks

Only stout beer will do.

Dessert

Millefeuille served with ice cream.

Serves 4

PAUPIETTES DE BOEUF COTE D'AZUR

Beef olives Riviera style

Ingredients

2 sirloin steaks, 2.5 cm/1 inch thick
45 ml/3 tbsp oil for shallow frying

For the stuffing:
50 g/2 oz/¼ cup cream cheese
1 egg, beaten
30 ml/2 tbsp white breadcrumbs
8 large olives, stoned and chopped
1 clove of garlic, chopped
Flour for coating

For the sauce:
150 ml/¼ pint/⅔ cup Madeira wine
1 shallot, chopped
1 sprig of thyme
150 ml/¼ pint/⅔ cup Brown Sauce (page 20)
Salt and pepper

Method

1. Remove the fat from the sirloin steaks and, with a wooden mallet, beat the steaks to enlarge them to twice their size, like escalopes.

2. In a bowl, cream the cheese with the beaten egg. Add the breadcrumbs, olives and garlic. Spread the mixture thinly over each steak. Roll up the steak and tie with two strings at each end. Coat the steaks in flour.

3. Heat the oil in a frying pan and fry the steaks all over for 5 minutes until brown. Remove the steaks and surplus oil. In the same pan, boil the Madeira wine, shallot and thyme until reduced by half. At this stage, add the brown sauce and boil for 1 more minute. Strain and season.

4. Place the steaks and sauce in a shallow ovenproof dish. Cover and braise in a preheated oven at 180°C/350°F/gas mark 4 for 30 minutes. When cooked, remove the strings and serve with grilled (broiled) tomatoes, mushrooms and a green side salad.

Wines

Corbières, Bergerac or dry Rosé de Provence.

Dessert

Poires Doyenne du Comice au Beaujolais (page 128).

Serves 2

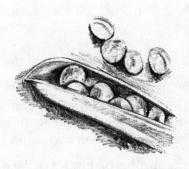

5 ENTRECOTE STEAK AU ROQUEFORT

Fried steak with Roquefort sauce

This is one of my specialities I used to feature in my own family restaurant many years ago. It has become fashionable on both sides of the Channel by younger chefs. They use different types of blue cheese from the very mild Italian Dolcelate to heavy Gorgonzola, often forgetting that French Roquefort and Danish blue taste better.

Ingredients

2 entrecôte steaks, 2.5 cm/1 inch thick
Black pepper
Oil for frying

For the sauce:
25 g/1 oz/¼ cup Roquefort cheese
25 g/1 oz/2 tbsp butter
75 ml/3 fl oz/6 tbsp dry white wine
50 ml/2 fl oz/¼ cup double (heavy) cream

Method

1. Blend the Roquefort cheese and butter to a paste.

2. Season the steaks with pepper only. Heat the oil in a frying pan and cook the steaks until medium or underdone, according to taste. Remove from the pan and keep them hot on two plates.

3. Remove the surplus oil but leave the meat juices. Add the wine and cream and boil for 3 minutes.

Add the Roquefort paste and stir until a creamy
consistency. Check seasoning and coat the steaks
with the sauce. Serve with Pommes Lyonnaise
(page 108) and Aubergine (eggplant) Frites
or beans.

Wines

Château Neuf-du-Pape or Fleurie.

Dessert

Apple Pie.

Serves 2

6 TOURNEDOS AU POIVRE VERT

Fillet steak with green pepper sauce

Some people prefer their fillet steaks plainly grilled and served with tomatoes, mushrooms and pommes frites. Although fillet is the most tender part of the beef, it has not as good a flavour as rump steak. For this reason, mustard and Worcestershire sauce are often used to flavour it as well as lots of black pepper. Gourmets have discovered the subtle flavour of green peppercorns which is only available in U.K. in tins. A sauce made with this pepper is so good that many cooks use it for fried liver or kidneys.

Ingredients

2 fillet (filet mignon) steaks, 150 g/5 oz each
30 ml/2 tbsp oil and butter for shallow-frying

For the sauce:
100 ml/4 fl oz/½ cup medium sherry or Madeira wine
15 ml/1 tbsp green peppercorns and as much of its juice
100 ml/4 fl oz/½ cup single (light) cream
Salt
Ground mace

Method

1.   Flatten the steaks with a rolling pin to a thickness of 1 cm/½ inch.

2.   Heat the oil and butter in a shallow frying pan and pan fry the steaks according to requirement – underdone, medium or well done. (3 minutes for underdone, 5 for medium and 8 for well done.) Remove the steaks and keep hot on a flat dish.

3.   Remove some of the oil. Add the sherry to the pan juices and deglaze for 2 minutes to reduce and increase flavour. Add the green peppercorns and its juice and the cream. Boil for 2 more minutes. Season with salt and mace and pour the sauce over the steaks. Serve with plain sauté potatoes and French beans.

Wines

Good Burgundy wines, Givry, Chinon or Chambertin.

Dessert

Chocolat Parfait.

Serves 2

7 BIFSTEAK SAUCE MOUTARDE

Rump steak in mustard sauce

While the whole French nation of steak eaters, young and old, thrive on underdone steaks from tougher cuts, the British beef-eaters love their beef underdone but use better cuts of meats.

Barbecue al fresco meals have become very popular in Britain, weather permitting, so here is a recipe using this way of cooking steaks with a selection of popular spicy sauces.

Ingredients

1 kg/2¼ lb piece of rump steak, 2.5 cm/1 inch thick
Oil for brushing

For the barbecue marinade 1:
30 ml/2 tbsp soya oil
1 clove of garlic, chopped
1 piece of fresh ginger
1 piece of green chilli, chopped
5 ml/1 tsp mustard powder
15 ml/1 tbsp oil
Juice of 1 orange
5 ml/1 tsp sugar or honey
5 ml/1 tsp ground mixed spice

For the barbecue marinade 2:
150 ml/¼ pint/⅔ cup port
2 shallots, chopped
15 ml/1 tbsp Dijon mustard
30 ml/2 tbsp oil
Salt and pepper

For the barbecue marinade 3:
100 ml/4 fl oz/½ cup fresh pineapple juice
15 ml/1 tbsp vinegar
15 ml/1 tbsp honey
1 grilled chilli, chopped
1 piece of ginger, chopped
2 cloves of garlic, chopped
30 ml/2 tbsp oil
45 ml/3 tbsp tomato ketchup

For the French mustard sauce:
100 ml/4 fl oz/½ cup White Sauce (page 22)
50 ml/2 fl oz/¼ cup sour cream
15 ml/1 tbsp Dijon mustard
5 ml/1 tsp chopped fresh tarragon
Salt and pepper

Method

1. All the barbecue sauces can be prepared in advance and bottled. Just blend them to a thin purée sauce. If more liquid is required, just top up with soya sauce. These barbecue sauces are just marinades but can be used as condiments like ketchups.

2. For the mustard sauce, simply blend the white sauce, cream and made mustard with the chopped tarragon. Season. This sauce can be reheated in a small saucepan over the hot barbecue.

3. Soak the rump steak in one of the barbecue marinades for 1 hour.

4. Light your charcoal fire and leave until amber without smoke. Have a wooden board and carving knife, slicer and a spoon on the table close to your barbecue.

5. When ready to cook, dry the steak and put it on the

barbecue grid. Brush with oil on both sides as you turn it over. Boil the barbecue sauce for 5 minutes, then strain.

6. Pass the barbecue sauce around to the guests to help themselves. Carve the rump steak in slices across like a joint into thin slivers. Place on a plate and accompany with a baked potato, slit open and filled with a pat of butter. Alternatively, thick French Pommes frites can be reheated in foil over the barbecue. See different cuts of Pommes frites in Savoury Vegetables (page 104). A variety of salads can also be served with barbecue meals.

Wines

Small barrel of wines can be put on taps using ordinary regional wines or use wine boxes; Corbières, Fitou, Cabernet Savignon.

Serves 4

8   ESTOUFFADE DE BOEUF ET ROGNON AU PORTO

Beef and kidney stew

One of the stews which emulates Boeuf Bourguignon is this kind of casserole using ox kidney and shin of beef.

Ingredients

> *450 g/1 lb shin of beef (shank), cut in 2.5 cm/1 inch cubes*
> *225 g/8 oz ox kidney, cut in thin slices*
> *1 carrot, cut in very small cubes*
> *1 stalk of celery, diced*
> *1 medium onion, chopped*
> *1 sprig of thyme*
> *600 ml/1 pint/2½ cups port*
> *Salt and black pepper*
> *5 ml/1 tsp gravy granules*

Method

1. In a bowl, combine all the ingredients except the gravy granules. Leave to marinate for 2 hours.

2. Place all the ingredients in a casserole. Cover the casserole tightly with a lid sealed with a flour and water paste. Braise in a preheated oven at 180°C/350°F/gas mark 4 for 1½ hours.

3. When ready, remove the lid and strain the liquor into a small pan. Add the gravy granules and boil for 3 minutes. Add to the cooked meat and vegetables. Serve with new boiled potatoes or shell pasta.

Wines

Red Burgundy, Macon or Beaune.

Dessert

Crème aux Cerises (page 142).

Serves 4

9 BOEUF EN CROUTE TOUT PARIS

Fillet of beef baked in pastry

Since this very French dish was created at the time of Napoleon in Paris for the celebration of the birth of his ill-fated son, the recipe crossed the Channel after Waterloo and the battle of Trafalgar, and reached much more popularity under Wellington. Apart from all this Boeuf en croûte is a very good dish for a celebration birthday dinner.

Ingredients

1 kg/2¼ lb piece of trimmed fillet of beef (filet mignon)
Salt and pepper
Oil for frying
4 large 16 cm/6½ inch cooked pancakes
700 g/1½ lb puff pastry
Flour for dusting
2 egg yolks for glazing
300 ml/½ pint/1¼ cups Madeira and Mustard Sauce (page 72)

For the liver paste:
45 ml/3 tbsp oil for frying
100 g/4 oz piece calf's liver
2 shallots, chopped
4 large mushrooms, chopped
30 ml/2 tbsp chopped fresh parsley
30 ml/2 tbsp double (heavy) cream
30 ml/2 tbsp breadcrumbs

Method

1.   Season the fillet with salt and pepper. Heat oil in a

metal shallow roasting tray and cook the meat on top of the cooker for 6-8 minutes to brown it all over. Transfer to a preheated oven at 240°C/475°F/gas mark 9 for 10 minutes. Remove the joint and cool for 2 hours.

2.	Prepare a liver paste to spread over the beef. Heat the oil in a frying pan and stir-fry the liver, shallots and mushrooms together for 5 minutes. Remove from the heat and mince the mixture to a fine paste. Add the parsley, a little cream and the breadcrumbs. Use to coat the fillet of beef evenly. The alternative is to use a liver pâté already made, such as Pâté de Foie.

3.	Wrap the fillet with the pancakes like a parcel.

4.	Dust flour on a pastry board and roll out the puff pastry into a rectangle longer than the length of the fillet. Place the fillet on the pastry. Brush all round with water and tuck each end under like a neat parcel in a cylindrical shape. Place the meat onto a greased baking tin. Brush the top with egg yolk and rest for 20 minutes.

5.	Bake in a preheated oven at 200°C/400°F/gas mark 6 until golden brown. Serve with Madeira sauce and small roasted potatoes, French beans or mangetout (snow) peas. Carve the meat in thick slices.

Wines

Château Neuf-du-Pape, Chambertin or Macon.

Dessert

Soufflé aux Pommes (page 140).

Serves 6

10 POT AU FEU DE BOEUF A LA FRANCAISE

Beef hot pot

Of all the traditional popular beef dishes, the French pot au feu is the most appreciated of our typical country meals. This once-a-week meal gives the most nourishment and least bother to the cook. It produces a meat and three vegetables as well as one of the most concentrated clear soups, so strong that it has become the basic stock that no convenience stock cubes can ever emulate. The choice of meats is varied from brisket, thin flank, rib top; silverside is the least fatty. The meat should be tied up with string.

Ingredients

1 kg/2¼ lb piece silverside
One small shin (shank) bone, cut open
1 onion, studded with 3 cloves
1 bouquet garni, made up of thyme and celery stalk
6 black peppercorns, crushed
3 litres/5¼ pints/6¼ pints water
6 medium carrots
6 medium turnips
6 medium leeks
20 g/¾ oz salt

Method

1.   Place the meat, bone, onion, bouquet garni and peppercorns in a very large stock pot and cover with the water. Bring the water to the boil and

simmer gently for 1½ hours, removing the scum as it rises from time to time until the broth is clear.

2. Add the carrots and turnips to the stock after the beef has simmered for 1½ hours.

3. Trim and clean the leeks and tie them up in a bunch. Cook the leeks after the beef has simmered for 2 hours, allowing only 10 minutes in the beef stock.

4. When all the ingredients are cooked, remove the meat and untie it. Remove the vegetables and drain over a colander. Remove surplus fat from the broth and season. Strain the broth. Place the meat in a shallow dish with 450 ml/¾ pint/2 cups broth to keep hot and place the vegetables in another dish. Keep hot.

5. Meanwhile, serve the broth in a terrine with sippets of bread separately for the first course of the meal as clear soup. Any surplus broth can be frozen for use in soups or sauces.

6. To serve the Pot au Feu: place one slice of beef, 1 carrot, 1 turnip and 1 white of leek on each plate. New boiled potatoes can be included as an accompaniment. Special condiments are usually served with Pot au Feu, such as pickled cucumber or gherkins, pickled cauliflowers, various chutneys and made mustards.

Wines

Regional red wines, Beaujolais, Fitou or Cabernet Sauvignon.

Dessert

Tranche aux Noisettes (page 148).

Serves 6

ESCALOPE DE VEAU CORDON BLEU

Veal escalope stuffed with ham and cheese

The taste of this veal escalope will depend on the type of cheese and ham selected for the filling. Gruyère, Port Salut, Cantalor even crustless Brie and Camembert or blue cheeses could be used. The best boiled ham or smoked ham will produce a different flavour.

Escalopes can be taken from the leg part – thick rump, or cushion of veal or even from the loin or veal fillet.

Ingredients

2 veal escalopes (scallops), 100 g/4 oz each
Salt and pepper
2 thin slices of cooked ham or bacon, 75 g/3 oz each
2 thin slices of hard or semi soft cheese, 50 g/2 oz each
60 ml/4 tbsp seasoned flour
2 eggs, beaten
100 g/4 oz/1 cup dry white breadcrumbs
Oil for shallow frying
8 asparagus tips or 225 g/8 oz mangetout (snow) peas

For the sauce:
150 ml/¼ pint/⅔ cup Brown Sauce (page 20)
45 ml/3 tbsp red port wine

Method

1.   Using a wooden mallet, flatten one veal escalope very thinly to twice its size in a rectangular shape.

Season. Place a slice of ham in half of the rectangle and a slice of cheese on top. Fold the veal escalope and gently tap it with the mallet without breaking the meat. Repeat the same operation with the other escalope.

2. Coat each escalope in seasoned flour, then in beaten egg. Toss in breadcrumbs on both sides.

3. Heat the oil in a shallow pan and pan fry the coated escalopes for 2 minutes on each side. Drain the escalopes on absorbent paper. Place in a dish and keep hot, while finishing the sauce.

4. Boil the brown sauce with port wine for 3 minutes. Check seasoning. Serve either or both the asparagus and mangetout peas with the sauce in a separate jug.

Wines

Muscadet or Chablis.

Dessert

Sabayon Grand Marnier.

Serves 2

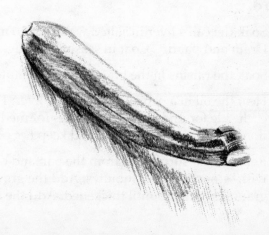

12 FOIE DE VEAU AUX RAISINS

Calf's liver with raisins

Calf's liver is the most tender and popular offal, much preferred than the liver from any other animal. It is also the most expensive after goose liver. Most gourmets like liver underdone; this is a question of taste but the longer it is cooked the tougher it will become.

Ingredients

2 slices of calf's liver, 150 g/5 oz each
Seasoned flour for coating
50 g/2 oz/⅓ cup seedless raisins
30 ml/2 tbsp brandy
Oil for frying
100 ml/4 fl oz/½ cup dry white wine
2.5 ml/½ tsp gravy granules
Salt and pepper
30 ml/2 tbsp chopped fresh parsley

Method

1. Soak the calf's liver in salted water for 10 minutes. Drain and pat dry. Coat in seasoned flour.

2. Soak the raisins in the brandy for 10 minutes.

3. Heat the oil in a pan and pan fry the liver; 1 minute each side for underdone, 3 minutes for medium done. Remove from the pan and keep hot on a dish.

4. Remove the surplus oil from the pan and deglaze with wine. Boil for 2 minutes. Add the gravy granules and stir until thickened. Add the raisins

in brandy and boil for 30 seconds. Season to taste. Sprinkle with parsley. Serve the liver and raisins with sauté potatoes and broccoli or peas.

Wines

Château Neuf-du-Pape, Nuits St George or Beaune.

Dessert

Meringue à la Crème (page 136).

Serves 2

COGNAC

13 ROGNON DE VEAU A LA DIJONNAISE

Calf's kidney sauté in Madeira and mustard sauce

Gourmets prefer calves' kidneys to ox or lamb because they are more tender. This celebrated kidney dish is often cooked in the dining room by chefs or head waiters as one of the flambé dishes. It is a light entrée which requires no garnish. It could be served with rice or as a filling for pastry cases (vol-au-vents). Once the kidneys have been sautéed and the sauce completed, they must not stew in the sauce more than a few seconds as they will toughen.

Ingredients

1 whole calf's kidney
Salt and pepper
Flour
15 ml/1 tbsp oil
15 ml/1 tbsp butter
45 ml/3 tbsp brandy
100 ml/4 fl oz/½ cup Madeira wine
2 shallots, chopped
50 g/2 oz/½ cup white mushrooms
1.25 ml/¼ tsp gravy granules
90 ml/6 tbsp double (heavy) cream
5 ml/1 tsp Dijon mustard

Method

1.   Remove the fat and sinews from the kidney and cut in thin slices. Coat in seasoned flour.

2. Heat the oil and butter in a shallow pan and quickly sauté the kidneys for 5 minutes. Add the brandy and ignite (optional). Add the Madeira wine, which extinguishes the flames, and cook for 30 seconds. Remove the kidney with a slotted spoon. Add the shallots and mushrooms and cook for 1 minute. Remove. Add the gravy granules to the pan.

3. Boil the liquid and add the cream, stirring. Season to taste and add made mustard with a quick stir. Do not boil the sauce. Reheat the kidney and vegetables in the mixture for 1 minute without boiling and VOILA! Serve on its own or with rice or new boiled potatoes.

Wines

White wines, such as Muscadet, Sancerre or Macon Blanc.

Dessert

Poire Belle Hélène (page 130).

Serves 2

14 ROULADE DE PORC NORMANDIE

Pork rolled meat with apple

Ingredients

225 g/8 oz/1 cup fresh lean minced (ground) pork
50 g/2 oz/½ cup peeled apple, chopped
1 egg
1 small onion, chopped
2 cloves of garlic, chopped
45 ml/3 tbsp chopped fresh parsley
45 ml/3 tbsp breadcrumbs
Salt and pepper

For the pastry:
50 g/2 oz/¼ cup margarine
225 g/8 oz/2 cups bread flour
1 egg
30-45 ml/2-3 tbsp water

Method

1. In a bowl, blend the meat, apple, egg, onion, garlic, parsley and breadcrumbs. Season to taste.

2. Prepare the pastry wrapping. In a bowl, rub the margarine into the flour with a pinch salt. Blend in the egg with sufficient water to make a soft dough. Knead well. Rest for 15 minutes.

3. On a floured board, roll the meat to a 2 cm/¾ inch cylindrical shape, like a thick sausage. Cut two strips of meat, 30cm/12 inches long. Place the strips on a floured tray and freeze for 1 hour to firm the meat.

4. Meanwhile on a floured board, roll out the pastry as thinly as possible, 3-4 mm/⅛ inch thick, and to a rectangle, 30 x 20 cm/12 x 8 inch. Cut in half lengthwise.

5. Place a strip of sausage meat onto the pastry and wrap the pastry around, sealing the ends with cold water. Repeat this procedure until all the meat is used, making two long rolls. Cut the meat rolls 7.5 cm/3 inches long to look like sausages.

6. There are two ways to cook: Either heat the oil in a shallow pan and deep fry the sausages for 3 minutes until golden. Transfer to a baking tray and bake in a preheated oven at 200°C/400°F/gas mark 6 for 5 minutes. Or bake them longer for 15-20 minutes. Served hot with pommes frites (page 104) and salad, this is a super snack meal.

Wines

Beaujolais, Vin de Touraine or Normandy cider.

Dessert

Fresh Raspberries in Wine.

Serves 4

15 FEUILLETE DE JAMBON AUX CHAMPIGNONS

French ham pie with mushrooms

Ingredients

225 g/8 oz made puff pastry
150 g/5 oz cooked bacon or ham, cut in thin slices
1 shallot, chopped
6 white mushrooms, sliced
30 ml/2 tbsp chopped fresh parsley
45 ml/3 tbsp chopped pickled gherkins (dill pickles)
150 g/5 oz Gruyère cheese, cut in thin slices
Flour for dusting
1 egg yolk for glazing

Method

1. On a floured board, roll out the pastry to a rectangle, 30 x 15 cm/12 x 6 inches. Divide into two equal pieces. Oil a baking tin and place one piece of pastry on it. Brush with water.

2. Cut the bacon or ham in small pieces. Lay them in the centre of the pastry strip. Sprinkle the chopped shallot, mushrooms, parsley and gherkins over, then cover with slices of cheese. Finally top with the other pastry strip. Crimp the edges and mark few slits on top. Brush with egg yolk and leave to rest for 1 hour.

3. Bake in a preheated oven at 200°C/400°F/gas mark 6 for 20 minutes. Cut in portions and serve hot or cold with an endive salad.

Wines

Light regional wines such as Beaujolais, Corbières or Cahors.

Dessert

Compote of assorted fruits.

Serves 6

16 GIGOT D'AGNEAU BRETONNE

Roast leg of lamb with mixed beans

Have the pelvic and chump bone removed from the leg by your butcher.

Ingredients

2 kg/4½ lb leg of lamb
3 cloves of garlic, cut in small slivers
Salt and pepper
75 ml/5 tbsp oil and butter, mixed
Lamb bones

For the gravy:
1 large onion, sliced
1 stalk of celery, sliced
1 large carrot, sliced
1 bunch rosemary
450 ml/¾ pint/2 cups water
15 ml/1 tbsp gravy granules

For the garnish:
450 g/1 lb French beans, trimmed
Canned flageolet beans
60 ml/4 tbsp butter
Salt and pepper

Method

1. Make several slits in the lamb with the point of a knife and insert slivers of garlic. Rub with salt and pepper. Brush with the oil and butter.

2. Place in a tray on a trivet of bones. Roast in a preheated oven at 200°C/400°F/gas mark 6 for 1½ hours, basting from time to time. Turn the leg over half way for even cooking.

3. At this stage, remove all surplus lamb fat. Add the onion, celery, carrot, rosemary and water. Reduce the heat to 190°C/375°F/gas mark 5 and cook for another 30 minutes.

4. When cooked, rest the meat but keep it warm. Prepare the gravy by boiling the liquid with the vegetables and rosemary, adding the gravy granules. Season to taste. After 10 minutes, strain the gravy. To carve, slice horizontally holding the shin bone. Then turn the leg over and repeat.

5. Boil the green beans for 8 minutes. Drain. Reheat the flageolet beans in its liquid and drain. In a saucepan, combine the two vegetables with the butter. Season and serve with the lamb, with roast or sauté potatoes.

Wines

Good claret wines, Medoc, St Julien, St Emilion, St Estephe, all the good saints of the Bordeaux region.

Dessert

Apple and Currant Pie.

Serves 8

17 CARRE D'AGNEAU POMMES BOULANGERE

Roast rack of lamb

Make sure to ask your butcher to prepare the best end of lamb with seven ribs – with fat and bark, cartilage, paddywax gristle, blade bone removed; tip of ribs trimmed and chine bone removed completely.

Ingredients

Salt and pepper
1.25 kg/2½ lb rack of lamb, trimmed and chined
5 ml/1 tsp dried mixed herbs
Lamb bones
Oil for cooking
1 medium onion, sliced
450 g/1 lb potatoes, peeled and thinly sliced
50 g/2 oz/¼ cup butter

For the gravy:
1 small onion, sliced
100 ml/4 fl oz/½ cup water
100 ml/4 fl oz/½ cup white wine
5 ml/1 tsp gravy granules

Method

1. Season the rack of lamb and rub herbs and seasoning on the fat part. Place in a roasting tray with a few bones.

2. Heat 45 ml/3 tbsp oil in a frying pan and pan fry

the 2 sliced onions until pale colour. Remove. Keep just under half for the gravy and the remainder for the potato dish.

3.   Arrange a layer of onions in an earthenware dish and cover with sliced potatoes. Spread with small pieces of butter and seasoning. Pour a cup of water over the potatoes.

4.   Bake the two dishes in a preheated oven at 200°C/400°F/gas mark 6 for 30 minutes.

5.   Reduce the heat to 150°C/300°F/gas mark 2 to keep the potatoes hot. Place the lamb over the potatoes. Remove all the fat from the roasting tray. Pour the juices into a saucepan. Add the remaining fried onion, water and the wine. Boil for 5 minutes and thicken with the gravy granules. Boil for 1 minute more. Season to taste. Strain.

6.   Serve the sauce separately with a jug of mint sauce and one of redcurrant jelly. Divide the rack into cutlets. Serve with the potatoes, spring greens; sprouts or broccoli would go well with this lamb dish.

Wines

Red Claret, Pauillac or Medoc.

Dessert

Gâteau au Fromage Frais Citrone (page 146).

Serves 2

18 TITAN D'AGNEAU PROVENCALE

Lamb and aubergine pie

Most supermarkets and butchers sell minced lamb.
The making of such pies is better with raw meat
than mincing left-over roasted meats. This delicious
mixture of provençal vegetables adds to the
piquancy of this popular pie.

Ingredients

450 g/1 lb/2 cups minced (ground) lamb
1 egg, beaten
2 cloves of garlic, chopped
30 ml/2 tbsp chopped fresh parsley and basil
Salt and black pepper

For the garnish:
1 aubergine (eggplant)
1 courgette (zucchini)
1 large tomato
1 medium onion
1 medium potato, peeled and thinly sliced
60 ml/4 tbsp olive oil

Method

1. In a bowl, combine the minced meat with beaten
    egg, garlic and herbs. Season with 1.25 ml/¼ tsp
    salt and a good pinch of black pepper. Line a deep
    earthenware dish, about 1.75 litre/3 pint/4 pint
    capacity, with the meat.

2. Slice the aubergine (eggplant) and soak in water
    for 10 minutes to eliminate the bitter juices. Rinse

off and pat dry. Slice the unpeeled courgette (zucchini). Make a slit in the tomato and scald in boiling water for 30 seconds. Skin and cut in half. Squeeze out the seeds and slice the pulp.

3. Arrange a row of aubergine over the meat, then onion, tomato and courgette. Top with potato slices, overlapping. Brush them with olive oil.

4. Bake in a preheated oven at 200°C/400°F/gas mark 6 for 30 minutes until golden brown. After 15 minutes, press the mixture with a slicer. This delicious pie can be eaten hot on its own or cold with green salad.

Wines

Rosé de Provence, Carcassonne or Corbières.

Dessert

Strawberries and cream.

Serves 4

19 CASSOULET D'AGNEAU DE CARCASSONNE

Baked beans and lamb casserole

Nearly everybody eats baked beans from the age of five. There is no longer need to buy dry beans, and to have the long procedure to soak them overnight and cooking for two hours. Baked beans are in every supermarket for quick cooking. The combination of beans and lamb is perfect. In this century-old recipe I have cut corners in cooking time but the flavour is the same as the original, if not better.

Ingredients

45ml/3 tbsp oil
450 g/1 lb boneless stewing lamb
1 large onion, chopped
1 stalk of celery, sliced
600 ml/1 pint/2½ cups water
Salt and pepper
225 g/8 oz can baked beans
8 thin slices of garlic sausage
30 ml/2 tbsp grated cheese
2.5 ml/½ tsp basil
30 ml/2 tbsp breadcrumbs

Method

1.   Heat the oil in a heavy based pan and brown the meat for 8 minutes. In the same pan, stir fry the onion and celery. Cover with the water. Season to taste and simmer for about 45 minutes until the meat is tender.

2.   When the meat is cooked, drain the gravy into a saucepan. Add the baked beans and boil for 5 minutes.

3.   For Cassoulet presentation, you need two small round 600 ml/1 pint/2½ cup casserole dishes. Divide the meat between the casseroles. Using a slotted spoon, place some beans on top of the meat, add a little of the sauce, then the garlic sausage slices. Sprinkle grated cheese, basil and crumbs on top.

4.   Brown the two casseroles in a preheated oven at 200°C/400°F/gas mark 6 for 20 minutes. This dish needs no other accompaniment.

Wines

Sparkling white wine from the Loire Vallee.

Dessert

Figs in port wine.

Serves 2

Poultry

General Notes

A recent statistic on the consumption of popular dishes has shown that chicken, steak and salad are the first three favourite items in France, Italy and Britain.

Chicken is now big business. The housewives have a choice between free-range and battery products; the corn-fed chickens are certainly the best.

Quality varies according to breed, age, size and feeding. The flesh should be firm, the breastbone pliable, the breast fully-fleshed, and the skin bluish-white or yellow if corn fed, but not sticky and soft, and with no unbroken patches and no unpleasant smell.

Tenderness in birds is recognized by the pliability of the tip of the breastbone; if it is hard, the bird is sure to be old. Young birds can be recognized by the following features: 1. Small comb and wattles; 2. Smooth, pliable legs with bright scales; 3. Spurs not exceeding 2 cm (¾ inch); 4. White skin smooth to touch; 5. Soft and shiny feathers; 6. Soft bones.

Old birds (hardly sold in supermarkets) have well developed comb and wattles, hard, long legs, covered with coarse scale, long feathers which are hard to pull. They are only of use for soups and pies.

If you are given freshly killed poultry, they should be bled and hung in an aerated place for 24 hours before being plucked. Fresh poultry taste better than frozen birds.

Poultry is the general terms for the class of all domestic birds reared for cooking, i.e. chicken, turkey, goose, duck, guinea-fowl, pigeon; farm bred quail could be included.

Type	Age	Uses
Baby chicken	4-6 weeks	Grilling and roasting
Spring chicken	6 weeks	Grilling and roasting
Broiler	12-16 weeks	Grilling and roasting
Roaster	4-6 months	Roasting and sautéing
Capon	8 months	Pot roasting
Poularde	8 months	Poaching, boiling

Basic principle of roasting

The object in roasting is to sear the meat, keeping the succulent juices inside which when the bird is cooked right through should be clear with no sign of blood. If the chicken is overcooked no juice will be left and the poultry will be bland and dry. The bird must therefore be roasted quickly at high heat as slow cooking does not sear but dries the meat.

The first 10 minutes should be at the top temperature of 220°C/425°F/gas mark 7 then the cooking should be completed at 200°C/400°F/gas mark 6. Start the roasting by placing the bird on its side, leg downward. After ten minutes, turn it on the other side. Baste from time to time.

It is always best to roast a chicken in butter, oil or in chicken fat. It is the fat which picks up the flavour for good natural gravy. Fatty birds hardly require any additional oil or butter. Never remove the feet of roasters before they are cooked as they impart a good flavour as does the skin in all birds.

Gravy making

First of all wash the bird in salted water. Drain well and
dry. Season the inside and outside of the bird with salt prior
to roasting. Place half a medium onion, half a carrot and a
stalk of celery in the cavity of the bird ten minutes before
roasting.

When the chicken is cooked. Remove it but drain the
juices into the baking tray. Put the tray on top of the stove.
Remove any surplus fat but leaving at least 30 ml/2 tbsp.
Add 300 ml/½ pint/1¼ cups water. Season with black
pepper and boil quickly for 10 minutes. If the bird is large,
double the water.

If the gravy is not strong enough, add 5 ml/1 tsp chicken
granules or a stock cube.

Additional parts of the chicken, the giblets, such as neck,
winglets, gizzard (cleaned), can be used to produce gravy.
Boil them separately with an onion and celery stalk.

The gravy should be clear but if preferred a slight
thickening can be produced by adding a little cornflour
(cornstarch) diluted with cold water and added to the
boiling gravy. Usually 5 ml/1 tsp is enough for 600 ml/
1 pint/2½ cups gravy.

For duck, goose, guinea fowl or even turkey, add a glass
of port or medium sherry to the gravy. Or use fruit juices
such as apple, pineapple, orange or plum syrup.

Stuffing

Traditionally, stuffing is the perfect accompaniment.
Modern cooks prefer to bake it separately in an oblong tin
like a cake. Thus it is more presentable neatly sliced.

Chestnut stuffing

225 g/8 oz/1 cup pork sausagemeat, 100 g/4 oz cooked
chestnuts, 1 small onion, chopped, 30 ml/2 tbsp
breadcrumbs, 1 egg, salt and pepper. Combine all the
ingredients in a bowl. Grease a 600 ml/1 pint/2½ cup
capacity oblong tin and add the stuffing mixture. Bake at

the same time as the chicken for 20-30 minutes. Rest a little and turn out like a cake on to a clean board. Slice thickly and serve separately with the chicken. Apply the same cooking procedures for the following stuffings:

Ham and celery stuffing
225 g/8 oz/1 cup pork sausagemeat, 1 egg, 100g/4 oz/ ½ cup chopped cooked ham, 1 stalk of celery, chopped, 1 small onion, chopped, pinch of dried thyme, salt and pepper. Combine all the ingredients and cook like the Chestnut Stuffing in an oblong tin.

Sage and onion stuffing
225 g/8 oz breadcrumbs, 1 large onion, chopped and lightly fried in oil, pinch of dried sage, 15 ml/1 tbsp chopped fresh parsley, 1 egg, 30 ml/2 tbsp cream or cream cheese, salt and pepper. Combine and cook as the previous stuffings. (The egg keeps the stuffing in one piece.)

Liver and mushroom stuffing
Equal weight of sausagemeat, chicken liver, chopped, diced bacon, breadcrumbs – say 100 g/4 oz each. Add 1 egg, 1 small onion, chopped, 50-75g/2-3 oz white mushrooms, chopped, 1 clove of garlic, chopped, 15 ml/1 tbsp chopped fresh parsley, salt and pepper. Combine the mixture in a bowl and add 60 ml/4 tbsp brandy. Bake as above for 30 minutes. Slice like a cake. Serve with roast chicken or turkey.

Rice stuffing
Boil 100 g/4 oz long grain rice in 3 cups water for 17 minutes. Drain. Combine the cooked rice with a chopped boiled egg, 50 g/2 oz/⅓ cup seedless raisins and peanuts or almonds as required. Season with salt, black pepper and grated nutmeg or a pinch of saffron strands if liked.

Cooking duck
I spent two years as a creative chef, in the formulation of

duck recipes for one of the world's largest producers of ducks in Lincolnshire. Free-range ducks are less fatty than intensively fed birds which can be fattened up to 3 kg/ 6-7 lb. The surplus fat can be as much as 600 ml/1 pint/ 2½ cups per duck. Although the fat is a good medium for cooking potatoes, it is not of much use as an edible matter. Modern chefs frankly prefer to use wild duck varieties as they are the leanest and most flavoured. However, a good farm duck has its value in the hand of an experienced cook.

Pre-cooking procedure

1. Remove the back bone on both sides.

2. Cut off the flap of neck and discard as much fat as possible.

3. Scrape the collar bone and remove the wishbone (for easier carving after cooking).

4. Remove the winglet at humerus joint (upper arm). Prick the bottom part with a carving fork.

Cooking

1. Preheat the oven at 230°C/450°F/gas mark 8 for 15 minutes.

2. Place the duck on a tray or trivet of bones and winglets. Roast for the first 15 minutes at 200°C/ 400°F/gas mark 6; rest of time at 180°C/350°F/gas mark 4.

3. When cooked, drain the juices into a colander placed over a tray.

4. Allow more cooking time for ducks with more fat. Timing: 2 kg/4½ lb duck – 1½ hours
   2.5 kg/5½ lb duck – 1 hour 55 mins.

Carving

1.   Cut the breast by carving from the joint of the breastbone to the neck side. Carve the breast in thin slices.

2.   Remove the leg by lifting it out of its socket with a fork. Cut the leg in two, separating the thigh from the drumstick.

Gravy making

Remove as much fat as possible and in the tray use the juices as a base for flavour. Add a few cooked bones, winglets, 1 shallot and one sliced carrot. Cook these ingredients on top of the stove in the same roasting tray to reduce the juice to a glaze for 3-4 minutes. Add 300 ml/ ½ pint/1¼ cups water and boil for 10 minutes. Strain over a sieve or colander. Collect the gravy in a saucepan. Either thicken with a little cornflour (cornstarch) diluted with cold water added to the boiling gravy or just add 5 ml/1 tsp gravy granules for a quick gravy. Season with salt and black pepper. Pass the gravy through a fine strainer. Reheat in the saucepan. If liked, add 100 ml/4 fl oz/½ cup red or white port per 600 ml/1 pint/2½ cups gravy. Alternatively use the same amount of orange juice or cherry juice. The flavour can be enhanced with a pinch of chilli pepper.

ORANGE SAUCE FOR DUCK

Ingredients

3 sugar lumps
2 oranges
10 ml/2 tsp distilled vinegar
Juice of 2 oranges
600 ml/1 pint/2½ cups duck gravy
5 ml/1 tsp dried mint
10 ml/2 tsp cornflour (cornstarch)
Salt and black pepper
A pinch of cayenne pepper (optional)
1 glass of white port

Method

1. Rub the three lumps of sugar on the skin of an orange. Put them in a small saucepan, add the vinegar and heat until it turns copper brown caramel.

2. Add the orange juice and boil for 2 minutes. Add the gravy and mint. Boil for 3 minutes – the mint will enhance the orange flavour while losing its minty taste.

3. In a cup, blend the cornflour with a little water and add to the boiling sauce. Season with salt, pepper and cayenne pepper (optional). Strain and keep hot.

4. Peel and cut off the white skin from the two oranges, cut them into segments.

5.   With a rinder, grate one orange – about 30 ml/
2 tbsp zest. Boil the zest in water for 5 minutes.
Drain and add to the sauce with the white port.

6.   Place a duck portion on a plate and coat with
orange sauce. Arrange a few leaves of curly salad
and few segments of orange around.

Variation: Add a few stoned red Morello cherries.

2. COQ AU VIN BOURGUIGNONNE

Chicken sauté with wine

This well known chicken dish owes its popularity to the succulence of the flesh impregnated with wine. Strong wines are preferable but the addition of a glass of red port or brandy will give it a kick. For convenience, you can also use prepared chicken legs only.

Ingredients

1.5 kg/3½ lb chicken
60 ml/4 tbsp seasoned flour
Oil for shallow frying
2 rindless rashers (slices) of bacon, cut in pieces
450 ml/¾ pint/2 cups red wine, 12% volume
1 sprig of thyme
1 small stalk of celery
Salt and pepper
1.25 ml/¼ tsp ground cinnamon
30 ml/2 tbsp oil or butter
1 clove of garlic, chopped
12 small onions
12 button mushrooms
1 glass of red port or brandy (optional)

Method

1.   Remove the chicken legs and cut them in two, drumsticks and thigh apart. Cut off the knee caps. Cut the breast across in two or three pieces. Remove winglets which can also be used. Discard the neck flap of skin. Coat all the pieces in

seasoned flour (5 ml/1 tsp salt to 60 ml/4 tbsp flour). Shake off surplus flour by putting the pieces in a colander.

2. Heat the oil in a large shallow pan and fry the pieces all over for 8 minutes, turning the pieces as they become brown. Transfer the chicken to a casserole, 4.5 litre/8 pint/9 pint capacity.

3. Fry the bacon pieces for 2 minutes. Drain and add to the chicken with the red wine, the thyme, celery stalk and seasoning, including a good pinch of cinnamon.

4. Cover and braise in a preheated oven at 190°C/375°F/gas mark 5 for 40-45 minutes.

5. Heat the oil in a pan and stir fry the garlic, onions and mushrooms for 3 minutes. Drain and add to the chicken for 15 minutes before the chicken is cooked. At this stage check that the wine has not evaporated too much, add 1 small cup of water and one chicken stock cube if necessary. When ready, taste and add a pinch of black pepper and a glass of port wine or brandy if needed. Serve on a plate with a garnish of shell pasta or new boiled potatoes and baby carrots.

Wines

The same wine as in the chicken or a good Burgundy, Macon, Fleurie, Côtes de Beaune.

Dessert

Maids of Honour.

Serves 4

3   FRICASSEE DE POULET ROYAL

Chicken sauté à la king

A fricassée of this type is always a popular item for a wedding luncheon. It is usually served with rice.

Ingredients

4 chicken breasts, 225 g/8 oz each
60 ml/4 tbsp seasoned flour
60 ml/4 tbsp butter and oil mixed
1 sprig of thyme
1 stalk of celery, sliced
300 ml/½ pint/1¼ cups water
100 ml/4 fl oz/½ cup medium sherry
1 medium onion, chopped
1 red pepper, seeded and diced
8 white mushrooms, sliced
225 g/8 oz long grain rice
50 g/2 oz/¼ cup butter

For the thickening:
30 ml/2 tbsp butter
30 ml/2 tbsp flour
Grated nutmeg
150 ml/¼ pint/⅔ cup double (heavy) cream
Salt and pepper
Grated nutmeg

Method

1. Cut each breast of chicken in four or five pieces and rub in seasoned flour.

2. In a large sauté pan, 4.5 litre/8 pint/9 pint

capacity, heat half the butter and oil and fry the chicken pieces for 3 minutes, without browning. Add the thyme, celery, water and sherry. Bring to the boil gently and simmer for 10 minutes only. Drain the pieces in a colander over a bowl. Reserve the stock.

3. In the same shallow pan, heat the remaining butter and oil and stir fry the onion, red pepper and mushrooms for 2 minutes. Add the chicken pieces.

4. Prepare the sauce. In a small pan, boil the reserved chicken stock for 10 minutes to concentrate it. Cream the butter and flour for the roux paste. Add the stock, whisking to avoid lumps. Blend the cream, salt and pepper and grated nutmeg. Simmer for 8 minutes. Strain and pour over the chicken mixture. Reheat for 5 minutes without boiling.

5. Cook the rice in boiling salted water for 17 minutes. Drain and rinse in hot water. Drain again and dry in the oven for 10 minutes. Season and blend in the butter, stirring with a fork. Serve the chicken with the rice.

Wines

Dry sparkling white wines or dry Champagne.

Dessert

Tarte aux abricots (page 131).

Serves 6

4 VOL-AU-VENT A LA REINE

Cream chicken in pastry cases

Ingredients

225 g/8 oz quality made puff pastry

For the filling:
75 g/3 oz/¾ cup white mushrooms, diced
100 ml/4 fl oz/½ cup white port wine
150 ml/¼ pint/⅔ cup White Sauce (page 22)
60 ml/4 tbsp double (heavy) cream
Salt and pepper
Grated nutmeg
225 g/8 oz/1 cup cooked chicken breast or leg meat
without skin, diced

Method

1. On a floured board, roll out the pastry to 1 cm/
    ½ inch thick. With a pastry cutter 7.5 cm/3 inches
    in diameter, cut out four rounds.

2. Place the rounds on a lightly oiled baking tray and
    leave to rest for 30 minutes. With a smaller plain
    pastry cutter indent a smaller round, 5 cm/
    2 inches.

3. Bake in a preheated oven at 200°C/400°F/gas
    mark 6 for 12-15 minutes until well puffed up and
    golden. Remove the smaller round of pastry to
    make a cavity in each vol-au-vent case.

4. For the filling. Boil the mushrooms in the white
    port wine for 30 seconds. Add the white sauce and
    cream. Season to taste and reheat the cooked diced

chicken in this sauce for 5 minutes if chicken has just been cooked, or 15 minutes if it was cooked the day before. Alternatively, diced raw chicken can be sautéed for 10 minutes in butter or oil for freshness, then only reheated in the sauce. No garnish vegetables need be served with this kind of light entrée.

Wines

Alsace or Hock.

Dessert

Peach Compote.

Serves 4

CREPES DE VOLAILLE AUX POINTES D'ASPERGES

Chicken stuffed pancakes with asparagus

Ingredients

45 ml/3 tbsp butter
225 g/8 oz/1 cup raw chicken breast, without skin, diced
6 white mushrooms, diced
300 ml/½ pint/1¼ cups thick White Sauce (page 22)
50 g/2 oz/½ cup grated cheese
Salt and pepper
Grated nutmeg
4 small pancakes
8-12 cooked asparagus tips

Method

1. Heat the butter in a shallow pan and stir fry the chicken for 5 minutes until almost cooked. Add the mushrooms and cook for 2 minutes more. Remove any surplus fat and add the white sauce and half of the cheese. Season to taste. Boil for 5 minutes.

2. Place the pancakes on a clean board. Using a slotted spoon, fill each pancake with chicken mixture and roll them over. Place one pancake in an individual gratin dish. Coat the pancake with the remaining sauce mixture. Sprinkle with the remaining grated cheese.

3. Reheat in the oven for 10 minutes or under the grill (broiler) for 4 minutes. Top with two or three asparagus tips placed on top of each pancake. No other accompaniment needed.

Wines

Dry Graves, Chablis or White Macon.

Dessert

Tomato Sorbet.

Serves 4

Savoury Vegetables

General Notes

Although the French have not been converted yet to full vegetarianism as in Britain, the range of vegetables is greater than the meat repertoire of British cuisine. There are hundreds of ways to cook a potato, an onion or a carrot.

Leaf spinach or Swiss chard can be made into fillings for quiches and tarts. Meridional and Alsacian tarts are featured in the best restaurants, as are vegetables and cheese soufflés. Aubergines, tomatoes and courgettes can be made into ratatouille, hot or cold. The range of hors d'oeuvre salads too is immense, including mushrooms, black olive pâtés, globe artichokes, lentils in vinaigrette, French haricots verts served hot as garnish or in salads.

A nation which can produce 400 different cheeses could claim a share of the production of dishes for the world vegetarian nations. Thanks to Pasteur and Madame Curie, the French have discovered the need to safer foods through sterilization of milk. The use of wines in cooking is not only for flavouring purposes for alcohol kills germs as does vinegar.

Nutritionally, the need for sticking to a mixed diet has been approved by the most eminent scientists not denying that it is also beneficial to become vegetarian one day a week or during certain stages of one's life.

This being stated with much gallic excitement I like to think, as the author of a best vegetarian book, that now and then lots of vegetables will enhance many menus but not at the expense of cutting fish, meat or poultry.

In this section the number of vegetables and salads has to be limited for lack of space. In France we prefer to serve our main dishes with one item only either potatoes or pasta or pulses. We prefer the other vegetables, like peas, asparagus, lentils, leeks, to be served as a course on its own. There are exceptions when the meat course calls for several mixed vegetables, like boiled beef for instance.

The favourite accompaniments will remain for many years to come – Pommes frites with steaks; newly boiled potatoes with our stews; French beans with roast lamb; cabbage, cauliflower and spinach with pork and bacon; peas with duck; sprouts with turkey; grilled tomatoes and mushrooms with mixed grill; and green salads with every meal on its own with a plain dressing of good quality olive oil and wine vinegar.

In the order of popularity I will begin with Pommes frites and other deep fried vegetables.

1 POMMES FRITES

French fried potatoes

Size 7.5 cm/3 inches long, 6 mm/¼ inch thick is the standard.

The thinner kind is the same length but less thick 4 mm/⅛ inch and known as Pommes Allumettes.

The thicker potatoes are best blanched. Frying without colouration at 165°C/330°F and for last browning operation at 190°C/375°F.

Thin potato chips are cooked in one operation.

Method

1. Peel the potatoes, cut and trim ends. Cut the correct thickness and wash in cold water. Drain and pat dry on a cloth.

2. Heat the oil to 165°C/330°F and using a proper deep frying pan, make sure the oil is only half way up the sides as the oil might foam up, overspill and catch fire. First blanching will take 4 minutes. Drain well and store on a tray lined with a cloth or absorbent paper.

3. When ready to serve, heat the fat to 190°C/375°F and brown, within 1-2 minutes the chips will be ready. Drain well and season with salt.

Note: The amount of French fried potatoes depends on the requirement but usually 150-225 g/5-8 oz per person if it is the only vegetable served.

Frying medium

The type of oil used in deep frying makes an important contribution not only to the flavour but also to the diet of the individual. Polyunsaturated oils are used more now than before, when dripping and lard were considered to be the best for chips and fried vegetables. Corn, peanut and soya are best for frying. A good oil should have no flavour of its own.

The smoking point of a good oil should be 230°C/450°F. The flare point is about 160°C/325°F.
The correct temperature for deep frying is between 165°C/330°F and 190°C/375°F.

Frying tips

- For a large quantity of fried potatoes or fish, you will need a large deep frying pan, 4.5 litre/8 pint/ 9 pint capacity. You only fill the pan half full as the oil or fat rises when you add the chips.

- For sauté potatoes, use butter with a little oil mixed in.

- Olive oil is best for fish.

- The smaller the items the hotter the oil. A big piece of fish would require a lower temperature than chips.

2 MISTO FRITTO

Deep fried coated vegetables

Here is a collection of vegetables which can be
served as a Misto fritto or medley on their own.

Ingredients

Oil for deep frying
6 sprigs of parboiled cauliflower
1 aubergine (eggplant)
1 courgette (zucchini)
6 button mushrooms
225 g/8 oz/2 cups seasoned flour
3 eggs beaten with 100 ml/4 fl oz/½ cup milk
225 g/8 oz white breadcrumbs
100 g/4 oz sesame seeds
Lemon juice

Method

1. Heat the oil to 190°C/375°F. Dip the frying basket
   in hot oil, then arrange the first item to be fried.
   When completed, proceed to the next. (Begin with
   the vegetable which takes the longest to brown.)

2. For cauliflower fritters, parboil the cauliflower
   sprigs in salted water for 3 minutes. Drain well.
   Coat in seasoned flour, then beaten egg and finally
   in breadcrumbs. Deep fry for 2 minutes. Drain on
   absorbent paper.

3. For aubergine (eggplant) fritters, cut the aubergine
   across in 4 mm/⅙ inch slices. Sprinkle with salt
   and leave for 20 minutes. Rinse in cold water and
   pat dry in a cloth. Coat in seasoned flour, then
   beaten egg and lastly in sesame seeds. Deep fry for

1 minute. Drain on absorbent paper.

4.   For courgette (zucchini) fritters, cut the courgette in half across, then cut in quarters lengthwise in strips. There is no need to peel the courgette. Sprinkle with lemon juice. Coat in seasoned flour, then beaten egg and finally in breadcrumbs. Deep fry for less than 1 minute. Drain on absorbent paper.

5.   For mushroom fritters, peel the mushrooms as the batter will stick better. Coat in seasoned flour, then beaten egg and finally either breadcrumbs or seeds. Deep fry for 1 minute. Drain on absorbent paper.

6.   Serve the fritters as a garnish for roast poultry, fried veal escalopes or for cocktail parties with tartare sauce as a dip.

Serves 4-6

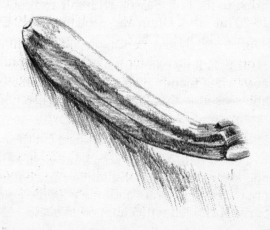

Boiled and Sautéed Vegetables

Many vegetables should be blanched or boiled before being shallow fried in as little oil and butter as possible. The use of butter provide a better flavour and when mixed it has a higher flash point. If left over a high heat the butter would burn.

3 POMMES LYONNAISE

Shallow fried sliced potatoes with onions

Ingredients

450 g/1 lb new potatoes
Salt and pepper
60 ml/4 tbsp butter and oil mixed
1 large onion, sliced
30 ml/2 tbsp chopped fresh parsley

Method

1. Put the potatoes in their skins in cold water and bring to the boil. Season with salt and cook for 15-20 minutes. Drain and cool, then peel. Cut into 5 mm/¼ inch thick slices.

2. Heat a shallow pan with half the oil and butter and, when foaming, add half of the potatoes, toss and season with salt and pepper. When golden, remove and keep on a tray lined with absorbent paper. Proceed the same for the next batch.

3. In a clean pan, heat the remaining butter and oil and stir fry the onion until uniformly golden but not too brown. Drain and mix with the potatoes. Serve sprinkled with chopped parsley.

Variation: For plain potatoes, omit the onion. You can sauté uncooked potatoes, without the boiling process, but they should be sliced thinner.

Serves 2

 # HARICOTS VERTS AU BEURRE

French kidney dwarf beans

Ingredients

450 g/1 lb best quality French beans, trimmed
60 ml/4 tbsp butter
Salt and pepper

Method

1. Cook the beans in a saucepan of boiling salted water for 5 minutes. Drain and refresh in iced water or cubes, to keep the green colour. Drain and pat dry.

2. Heat the butter until frothy and toss the beans for 2 minutes. Season with salt and black pepper. Serve with veal escalopes, roast or grilled lamb or chicken.

Serves 4

5 PETITS OIGNONS

Sauté button onions

Ingredients

450 g/1 lb button onions
30 ml/2 tbsp butter
15 ml/1 tbsp sugar
5 ml/1 tsp vinegar

Method

1. Scald the onions in a saucepan of boiling salted water for 30 seconds. Drain.

2. Heat the butter and stir fry the onions until golden. Add the sugar and allow to partially caramelize. Sprinkle over the vinegar and allow to evaporate. Serve hot or cold. (If larger onions are used, they should be boiled for at least 5 minutes, depending on the size.)

Serves 2

6 PETITS POIS A LA FRANCAISE

Peas French style

Ingredients

225 g/8 oz fresh peas
12 button onions
15 ml/1 tbsp butter
4 lettuce leaves, shredded
7.5 ml/½ tbsp butter blended with 5 ml/1 tsp flour
Salt and pepper
5 ml/1 tsp sugar

Method

1. Blanch the peas and button onions for 5 minutes, drain. Refresh under cold running water. Drain.

2. Heat the 15 ml/1 tbsp butter in a pan and stir fry the lettuce leaves for 2 minutes, add ½ cup water and reboil the peas and onions for 3 minutes. Stir the creamed butter and flour into the pan. Season with salt, pepper and sugar. Serve with duck.

Serves 2

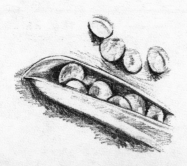

ROUNDELLES DE CAROTTES AU MIEL

Stir fried carrots in honey

This is probably the best recipe for carrots for freshness and taste.

Ingredients

450 g/1 lb medium carrots
30 ml/2 tbsp butter and oil mixed
1 shallot, finely chopped
15 ml/1 tbsp honey
5 ml/1 tsp anis seeds
5 ml/1 tsp wine vinegar
Salt and pepper
30 ml/2 tbsp chopped fresh parsley and coriander leaves

Method

1. Slice the carrots thinly slantwise.

2. Heat the butter and oil in a large frying pan and stir fry the carrots for 4 minutes. Add the shallot, honey, anis seeds and vinegar. Season to taste. Stir fry for another minute. Serve with chopped fresh parsley and coriander leaves. Serve with boiled beef, bacon or ham.

Serves 2

8 | POMMES SUZETTE

Jacket baked potatoes

Ingredients

2 large baking potatoes, 225 g/8 oz each
50 g/2 oz/¼ cup butter
Salt and pepper
60 ml/4 tbsp yoghurt
15 ml/1 tbsp snipped chives
Grated cheese

Method

1. Wash and dry the potatoes. With the point of a knife, make a groove around the potato lengthwise. (This will help when splitting the potato in two.) Wrap in foil and place on a baking tray. Bake in a preheated oven at 200°C/400°F/gas mark 6 for about 1 hour. This can be done at the same time as you roast a joint.

2. When done, remove the foil. Cut the potatoes in halves. Scoop the pulp into a bowl. Mash the pulp to a purée and pass it through a sieve if possible. Add the butter, salt and pepper, yoghurt and chives. Refill all the potato skins as if they were cases.

3. Sprinkle over some grated cheese and brown under the grill (broiler) for 3 minutes. Serve with pork chops or plain roast chicken.

Serves 2

9 GRATIN DE POMMES SAVOYARD

Baked potatoes in cream

Of all the potato dishes, this is one which has found favour throughout the ages. To avoid the potato curdling the cream during baking when baked raw, I suggest a quick scalding of the potatoes.

Ingredients

900 g/2 lb potatoes, peeled and sliced
50 g/2 oz/¼ cup butter
3 cloves of garlic, finely chopped
300 ml/½ pint/1¼ cups single (light) cream
Salt and pepper
Pinch of grated nutmeg
100 g/4 oz/1 cup mature Cheddar or Gruyère cheese, grated

Method

1. Bring a large saucepan of salted water to the boil. Place the sliced potatoes in a wire basket and scald for 3 minutes.

2. Sprinkle the bottom of a well buttered shallow dish with the chopped garlic. Arrange the sliced scalded potatoes overlapping on top.

3. Cover with the cream and season to taste, using 5 ml/1 tsp salt. Sprinkle with the grated cheese. Bake in a preheated oven at 200°C/400°F/gas mark 6 for 30 minutes until golden brown. You could use individual egg gratin dishes for better presentation.

Serves 6

Salads

Leaf Salads

The two main types are: cos, which are long with crisp leaves; and cabbage lettuces, which are further divided into smooth-leaved, globular butterheads and crinkly leaved crisp-heart iceberg types. In addition, there is the variety 'Salad Bowl' with leaves but no heart.

Some flavoured leaves include the lamb's lettuce known as corn salad, watercress and mustard and cress with a peppery taste, the curly endive and the Batavian larger leaves. The oak leaves and the variety of red chicory known as raddichio, and the white chicory often referred to in France as Belgian endive.

Winter salads include the leaves of white and green cabbages. Leaves and stems of celery and fennel and raw spinach leaves can also be used in salads, and some varieties of kale.

Vegetable and Fruit Salads

All roots, bulbs, seeds and pods make good vegetable salad ingredients, often bound in cream dressing or mayonnaise. Cooked potatoes and carrots, turnips, beans and peas are examples. All raw grated roots can also be used: beetroots, carrots, swedes, mooli and radishes. Cooked globe and Jerusalem artichokes are typical French salads. Mushrooms can be eaten raw as well as cooked in composite salads. Asparagus, sweetcorn, broccoli, peppers and aubergines (eggplants) as well as courgettes (zucchini) and marrow. In fact, the whole garden can be presented in a salad bowl, not forgetting tomatoes, small or large gherkins, cucumber and button onions.

The addition of citrus fruits, apples and pears, plums and peaches, pineapples, melons and pawpaws are all used in summer salads. There are great many salad combinations using all the various ingredients.

Salad Dressings

The basic dressing for most French salads is oil and vinegar with appropriate seasonings which include a little made mustard. This dressing is known as Vinaigrette.

There are different flavoured vinegars and oils on the market which gimmicky cooks might find interesting. Some use unsaturated oils namely olive, maize and corn oil but the most common oil used is made from ground nut and known as Arachide oil.

Fruit, herb and wine vinegars are also used but the plainer the flavour the better. Cider vinegar too is recommended.

On the nutritional basis, oil is a lubricant which helps the absorption of vitamin A in carrots, tomatoes and dark green vegetables. Vinegar or lemon juice helps to preserve vitamin C and make salads more acidic. Vinegar also helps kill germs; but not lemon juice. Herbal concoctions can also aromatize the salads using three well known anti-germ agents: onion, shallots and garlic.

Tarragon, basil, dill, parsley, anis seeds, fresh thyme, chive can be sprinkled over the salad or liquidized with the dressing.

When oil is substituted by cream, cooked white sauce, yoghurt, blue cheese paste or made mayonnaise, it becomes classified under salad cream dressings as opposed to vinaigrette.

1 SALADE NIÇOISE

Composite fish and vegetable salad

Ingredients

225 g/8 oz new boiled potatoes
225 g/8 oz fresh French beans, trimmed
1 small lettuce
225 g/8 oz can tuna
4 small tomatoes, sliced
1 green pepper, seeded and cut into rings
8 anchovy fillets
4 hard-boiled eggs, cut into wedges

For the dressing:
45 ml/3 tbsp wine vinegar
90 ml/6 tbsp olive oil
Salt and pepper

Method

1. Boil the new potatoes in their skins, peel and slice. Boil the beans for 8 minutes. Refresh and drain. Separate the lettuce leaves, wash and drain well.

2. On four large plates, place 3 lettuce leaves. In the centre, put the potatoes and top with a piece of tuna. Garnish with slices of tomatoes and pepper with anchovy fillets, flanked by green beans and hard-boiled egg wedges.

3. Mix the dressing ingredients and sprinkle it over the salad.

Serves 4

2 SALADE DE FLAGEOLETS PARISIENNE

Flageolet bean salad

Ingredients

150 g/5 oz dry flageolet beans

For the dressing:
60 ml/4 tbsp olive oil
30 ml/2 tbsp wine vinegar
2.5 ml/½ tsp Dijon mustard
15 ml/1 tbsp chopped shallot
1 clove of garlic, crushed
Salt and pepper
30 ml/2 tbsp chopped fresh parsley

Method

1. Soak the flageolet beans in distilled water overnight. Wash, then simmer in unsalted water for 1½-2 hours. Drain.

2. Combine the dressing ingredients in a salad bowl. Toss the hot cooked beans into this dressing. Serve hot or cold, with cold meat or roast pork.

   Note: Any kind of haricot (navy) beans, red or white, can be used similarly. The flageolet bean is slightly greenish and more tender.

Serves 4

3 VINAIGRETTE SAUCE

These ingredients are enough for 4 salads.

Ingredients

45 ml/3 tbsp olive or ground nut oil
15 ml/1 tbsp wine or distilled vinegar
½ tsp Dijon mustard
Salt and black pepper
Little finely chopped lemon rind

Method

1. Mix the ingredients together at the last minute. Alternatively, liquidize for a cream-like emulsion. It can be bottled and corked and kept refrigerated.

Variations

Cream Cheese
Use only 30 ml/2 tbsp oil and add 25 g/1 oz cream cheese.

Blue Cheese
Use only 30 ml/2 tbsp oil and add 25 g/1 oz blue cheese mashed with the vinegar.

White Sauce Dressing
Use only 15 ml/1 tbsp oil and add 45 ml/3 tbsp White Sauce (page 22) to dressing plus juice of ½ lemon.

Yoghurt Dressing
Omit the oil and blend yoghurt with vinegar or just lemon juice.

Fruit Juice Dressing
Replace the vinegar with one of the following fresh juices: pineapple, lemon, orange, grapefruit, tomato.

Egg Dressing
Emulsify 1 raw egg yolk with dressing.

Mayonnaise Dressing
Use 15 ml/1 tbsp mayonnaise instead of oil, using either vinegar, lemon or apple juice.

Nut Dressing
Mash up peanut butter in vinegar and omit the oil.

Cheeses

General Notes

In French gastronomy, cheese is served before the sweet not
the other way round as in England. Likewise the hot
savoury is a main feature served at the end of a meal
instead of a sweet but served with port wine.

In France we prefer to drink strong Burgundy wines with
our assorted platter of cheese:

Soft cheese: Cream, curd or herb
Fermented soft cheese: Brie or Camembert
Semi soft cheese: Port Salut, St Paulin, Gouda
Blue cheese: Roquefort, Danish Blue, Dolcelate,
Gorgonzola or Stilton
Hard cheese: Selection of Cheddar, Leicestershire,
Cheshire or Gruyère, Cantal or Dutch Edam

Vegetable crudités can be served with cheese, such as fennel,
carrots, cauliflower, celery, radishes, cucumber and tomato.

Serve cheese biscuits and crackers. The French prefer
eating a crispy baguette and cheese as a meal.

Selection of Cheese Recipes for Savouries

1 FROMAGE D'AVOCAT

Avocado cheese

Ingredients

100 g/4 oz/½ cup cream cheese
1 avocado, peeled and stoned
1 hard-boiled egg, chopped and sieved to a paste
1 shallot, chopped
Juice and grated rind of ½ lemon
30 ml/2 tbsp mayonnaise
Salt and black pepper

Method

1. Combine all the ingredients and pass through a sieve. Spoon the paste into 4 individual pots or ramekins. Serve with hot toast and carrot sticks.

Serves 4

2 | BOURSIN CHEESE

Herby cheese

Ingredients

225 g/8 oz/1 cup cream cheese
1 small sprig of thyme, chopped
2 cloves of garlic, chopped
30 ml/2 tbsp double (heavy) cream
Salt and black pepper

Method

1. Combine all the ingredients into a smooth paste. Store in a small pot covered with foil in the refrigerator. To be consumed within a week.

Serves 4

3 | BEIGNET DE BRIE AUX AMANDES

Brie cheese fritters

Ingredients

225 g/8 oz piece of Brie
Seasoned flour
1 egg, beaten
50 g/2 oz/½ cup flaked almonds
Frying oil

Method

1. Divide the Brie cheese in four wedges. Grate the

rind lightly. Pass the wedges in seasoned flour, then in beaten egg. Coat in flaked almonds. Heat the oil and fry the cheese fritters for about 1 minute until golden. Serve hot with slices of apple.

Serves 2

 # BAGUETTE GRATINEE

French stick snack

This is the quick and tasty pizza-like snack.

Ingredients

2 pieces of French bread baguettes, 20 cm/8 inches long, split lengthwise
60 ml/4 tbsp butter and olive oil mixed

For the topping:
225 g/8 oz cooked ham or raw smoked ham
2 large tomatoes, skinned, seeded and chopped
1 medium onion, sliced in rings
6 olives, stoned and chopped
5 ml/1 tsp made mustard
100 g/4 oz/1 cup Gruyère cheese, grated

Method

1. Toast the four halves of bread. Brush with melted butter and oil.

2. Top with a slice of ham, chopped tomato, rings of onion, olives, mustard and finally grated cheese. Place on a tray and brown under the grill (broiler) until the cheese is melted and golden brown.

Serves 2

Desserts

General Notes

The French love fresh fruits and lighter desserts more than
the British. The modern tendency is for open custard fruit
flans with less sugar than the original recipes demand. So
by definition French desserts include fresh fruits, compotes,
light jam galettes, crêpes, sorbets and, for formal occasions,
cream gâteaux, Caramel choux buns and the whole gamut
of soufflés and mousses.

Fresh fruits and nuts are basic desserts as well as items to
have with a cheese assortment.

Fresh and healthy! Isn't that the very essence of fruit's
appeal? In its various forms it brings us vitamin C when
eaten raw as cooking destroy this precious vitamin, and that
healthier, more slowly absorbed form of sugar called
fructose.

Naturally, many types of nuts are used in French desserts.
Almonds and hazelnuts are made into nougat and used in
powder form to flavour custard as the base of the best fruit
tarts and light French biscuits. Walnuts appear in mixtures

of sweet salads with apples and pears.

The most favoured sweets are still the meringues in various forms – Poached meringues with custards based on Oeufs à la Neige, Vacherin with whipped cream, the hot soufflés, the fruit tarts topped with light meringue.

Puff and short pastries and sponge flan cases can be bought and used to advantage to produce sweeter or more buttery taste for instance. This is done by sprinkling granulated sugar, ground almonds and cinnamon at the stage when the pastry is being rolled for flan or tarts. Another tip, after you have lined the pastry in the tin is to brush the inside with butter and sprinkle it with sugar.

Ideas for sweets and desserts have been mentioned at the end of meat and poultry recipes. Those with a page number are included in this section, others are not as there is no room to list the entire sweet repertoire of French desserts.

Wines with desserts

Without pontification on wines, it is traditional to serve sweet wines with most desserts. Such wines as Sauternes, Anjou and Rhine wines are by virtue of their taste recommended. With nuts and dry fruits it is the time for Port wines, Madeira and sweet sherry to be featured as well as being best with strong flavoured cheeses.

Dry Champagne is by far the best drink with the very rich meringue desserts and all types of ice cream desserts.

POIRES DOYENNE DU COMICE AU BEAUJOLAIS

Pears in wine syrup

Any of the pear varieties may be cooked when they are not fully ripe. However, they taste better if they are, and do not require long poaching in syrup. For this particular dessert I suggest ripe fruit, still firm.

Ingredients

6 ripe pears, Doyenne du Comice

For the syrup:
1 bottle of red Beaujolais
100 g/4 oz/½ cup granulated sugar
1 small stick of cinnamon
6 drops of red food colouring
60 ml/4 tbsp brandy

For the filling:
6 dried dates, stoned and chopped to a paste
15 ml/1 tbsp ground almonds

Method

1. Prepare the syrup. Place the wine in a stainless steel pan with the sugar and cinnamon. Bring to the boil and simmer for 5 minutes.

2. Make a paste of the dates and ground almonds.

3. Core and peel the pears. Fill the cavity with date paste. Immerse the pears in the wine syrup. Gently simmer (do not boil) for 4 minutes only if the pears

are ripe. If not, poach for 12 minutes. Transfer to a glass bowl.

4. Add few drops of red food colour to the syrup. Leave the pears to cool and marinate overnight. Serve in dessert plates with a little brandy added to the syrup. Serve with a sorbet, ice cream and almond shortbreads.

Note: In ripe pears, the poaching prevents the pears from fermenting, but the flavouring is obtained by marinating the pears in the syrup overnight to allow the liquid to penetrate the pears.

Serves 6

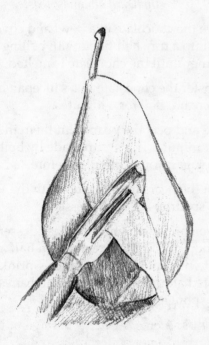

2 POIRE BELLE HELENE

Poached pears with chocolate sauce

Ingredients

> 100 g/4 oz dark chocolate, grated or cut in small pieces
> 100 ml/4 fl oz/½ cup double (heavy) cream
> 2 pears, Doyenne du Comice
> 300 ml/½ pint/1¼ cups water
> 100 g/4 oz/½ cup sugar
> Vanilla pod (bean) or essence
> 4 scoops dairy ice cream
> 50 g/2 oz/½ cup flaked almonds, toasted

1. Place the chocolate in a bowl and cover with foil. Put into a tray half filled with boiling water and simmer until the chocolate is melted.

2. Transfer the chocolate to a saucepan and blend in the cream. Boil for 4 minutes.

3. Core and peel the pears. Cut them in halves. Poach for 4 minutes in a syrup made by boiling the water and sugar from 2 minutes before.

4. Cool the pears in the syrup with the vanilla pod or add six drops of vanilla essence.

5. Presentation: on four flat glass dessert dishes place a scoop of dairy ice cream, then half a pear on top. Coat with hot chocolate sauce. Sprinkle with toasted almonds. Serve single cream separately and sponge (lady) fingers.

Serves 4

3 TARTE AUX ABRICOTS

Apricot tart

Ingredients

225 g/8 oz puff pastry

For the filling:
450 g/1 lb fresh apricots, stoned
100 g/4 oz/½ cup granulated sugar

For the confectioner's custard:
2 egg yolks
50 g/2 oz/¼ cup caster (superfine) sugar
50 g/2 oz/½ cup ground almonds
50 g/2 oz/½ cup cornflour (cornstarch)
300 ml/½ pint/1¼ cups milk

Method

1. On a pastry board dusted with flour, roll out the pastry to a round 4 mm/⅛ inch thick. Cut a round to fit a 23 cm/9 inch tart tin.

2. Oil the tart mould and line with the pastry round. Prick the bottom of the pastry with a fork all over. Arrange apricots closely together in one layer. Sprinkle with the sugar. Bake in a preheated oven at 200°C/400°F/gas mark 6 for 20 minutes.

3. Combine the egg yolks, sugar, ground almonds and cornflour. Bring the milk to the boil and stir the egg mixture in. Cook for 4 minutes, stirring until thickened. Remove from the heat.

4. After 20 minutes, remove the half baked tart. Pour over the custard and bake for 10 minutes until golden brown.

Serves 6

4 BEIGNETS DE POMME

Apple fritters with apricot sauce

Ingredients

4 apples, Golden Delicious or Granny Smith
100 g/4 oz/1 cup flour
5 ml/1 tsp ground cinnamon
Oil for frying
15 ml/1 tbsp icing (confectioner's) sugar

For the batter:
3 eggs
100 g/4 oz/1 cup strong flour
300 ml/½ pint/1¼ cups milk
Pinch of salt

For the apricot sauce:
50 g/2 oz/¼ cup granulated sugar
100 ml/4 fl oz/½ cup water
225 g/8 oz stoned fresh apricots
Juice of ½ lemon

Method

1. Prepare the apricot sauce first. Boil the sugar and water for 3 minutes and add the apricots. Boil for 4 more minutes. Add the lemon juice. Pass the mixture through a sieve or liquidize. This sauce is served cold.

2. Prepare the batter. Separate the egg yolks from the whites in two bowls. In a large bowl, mix the flour, milk, egg yolks and half of the whites. Beat the

remaining egg whites with the pinch of salt to a meringue. Fold into the batter. Rest for 10 minutes.

3.   When ready to serve, prepare the fritters. Core and peel the apples. Cut in thick rings. Mix the flour and cinnamon and use to coat each ring thoroughly.

4.   Heat the oil. Dip the floured apple rings in the batter and shake off the surplus. Deep fry for 1-2 minutes. Drain on absorbent paper and dust with sugar. Serve 4 rings per portion with apricot sauce separately.

Serves 4

5 CREME RENVERSEE AU CARAMEL

Caramel custard

Ingredients

100 g/4 oz/½ cup cubed sugar
4 medium eggs
75 g/3 oz/6 tbsp granulated sugar
6 drops vanilla essence
600 ml/1 pint/2½ cups milk

Method

1. Place six 150 ml/¼ pint/⅔ cup pyrex or metal moulds on a deep baking tray.

2. Put the sugar lumps in a saucepan, copper preferably, with 15 ml/1 tbsp water. Bring to the boil and cook for 3-4 minutes until it turns to copper colour. Immediately pour a little of the caramel onto the six moulds. It will harden within a minute. If you cook it longer the caramel will turn brown and taste bitter – so watch this operation. It is safer also to have a bowl full of ice cubes to cool the pan and stop the sugar cooking further after it has caramelized.

3. In a bowl, beat the eggs and granulated sugar, then add the vanilla essence and milk. Strain the mixture and fill the moulds coated with the caramel. Half fill the deep tray with hot water.

4. Bake in a preheated oven at 180°C/350°F/gas mark 4 for 20-25 minutes. To test that the cream is cooked, insert the point of a knife, if it comes out

clean without mixture attached to it, it is ready. (Take care, if the oven is too hot, the custard will puff up and the mixture will look like scrambled eggs.)

5.   Cool the cream and refrigerate for 3 hours, better still until the next day. This will melt the caramel; if consumed too soon the caramel will still be hard. Turn out on flat dessert plates and serve single cream separately.

Serves 6

MERINGUE A LA CREME

Baked meringue with egg custard and raspberries

Ingredients

For the meringue soufflé:
4 egg whites
Pinch of salt
225 g/8 oz/1 cup granulated sugar

For the custard:
4 egg yolks
50 g/2 oz/¼ cup sugar
2.5 ml/½ tsp cornflour (cornstarch)
6 drops of vanilla essence
4 drops of lemon essence
450 ml/¾ pint/2 cups milk

For the decoration:
225 g/8 oz fresh raspberries

Method

1. Coat six 150 ml/¼ pint/⅔ cup metal moulds with butter. Dust the insides with flour and invert the moulds, tapping them on the table to remove surplus.

2. Have a deep tray ready half filled with hot water.

3. In a clean grease-free bowl, place the egg whites and the pinch of salt or 5 ml/1 tsp lemon juice. This helps in coagulating the meringue. Using a balloon whisk or electric whisk, whisk the egg

whites until firm when it holds to the whisk. At this stage, add the sugar one dessertspoon at a time beating between each addition until the sugar is all used up and you have a firm meringue. Fill the moulds to the brim and place them in the tray.

4. Bake in a preheated oven at 180°C/350°F/gas mark 4 on the top shelf for 10-12 minutes until the meringue has puffed up and is firm. Remove and cool, then turn onto individual glass moulds, 200 ml/7 fl oz/1 cup capacity.

5. For the egg custard, in a metal bowl, beat the egg yolks and sugar for 5 minutes. Add cornflour and flavouring essences. Bring the milk to the boil and gradually pour it onto the egg yolks, whisking until well blended. Have a tray of water boiling and place the bowl in it. Whisk the mixture, while the water in the tray is boiling, until the custard thickens and coats the spoon.

6. At this stage, pour the custard over the meringue puddings to represent floating icebergs. Decorate with raspberries and serve cold.

Serves 6

7 VACHERIN AUX FRAISES

Meringue cake with cream and strawberries

Ingredients

For the meringue:
4 egg whites
5 ml/1 tsp lemon juice
225 g/8 oz/1 cup granulated sugar

For the filling:
300 ml/½ pint/1¼ cups whipping cream, chilled
50 g/2 oz/¼ cup granulated sugar
225 g/8 oz large strawberries, reserve a few for decoration
30 ml/2 tbsp flaked toasted almonds

Method

1. Grease two baking trays and line them with greaseproof (wax) paper. Brush melted butter or oil over the paper. Dust with flour and shake out the surplus by banging the tray upsidedown.

2. In a large grease-free bowl, place the egg whites. Add the lemon juice and beat with a balloon whisk or a mixer until the egg whites are firm like a meringue. At this stage, add the sugar, 15 ml/ 1 tbsp at a time, beating between each addition. The meringue should be firm.

3. Take a piping bag fitted with a large star tube (tip) and half fill it at a time with the meringue. Pipe a round on each tray starting at the centre and completing the round to 20 cm/8 inch diameter. If you have any surplus, overpipe the round.

4. Bake in a preheated oven at 150°C/300°F/gas mark 2 for 1½-2 hours, until the meringue is very dry, but not brown. Transfer one round of meringue onto a flat plate or round dish.

5. Whip the cream until thick, reserve some for the topping, then add the sugar. Spread the mixture thickly on the meringue cake. Add the strawberries. Put the other round of meringue on top. Press a little and, with a palette knife, coat more whipped cream around the edges. Spread the reserved plain whipped cream on top and sprinkle over flaked toasted almonds. Decorate with a few strawberries. Cut the Vacherin in six or eight portions using a bread knife.

Serves 6

8 SOUFFLE AUX POMMES

Apple soufflés

Ingredients

2 large cooking apples, cored, peeled and sliced, about
450 g/1 lb
30 ml/2 tbsp blackcurrant syrup
50 g/2 oz/¼ cup sugar
30 ml/2 tbsp Kirsch
10 ml/2 tsp cornflour (cornstarch) blended with 30 ml/
2 tbsp water
2 egg yolks
2.5 ml/½ tsp ground cinnamon
4 egg whites
Juice of ½ lemon
100 g/4 oz/½ cup granulated sugar

Method

1. Have ready four pyrex, ramekin soufflé dishes,
    capacity 200 ml/7 fl oz/1 cup. Oil with melted
    butter and dust with granulated sugar evenly.

2. Boil the apple with blackcurrant syrup, sugar and
    ½ cup water to a purée. Pass the purée through a
    sieve and reheat in another saucepan. Bring it to
    the boil. Add the Kirsch. Stir the blended cornflour
    and add it to the purée to thicken. Cook for
    4 minutes, stirring. Remove from the heat, transfer
    to a bowl and blend in the egg yolks and cinnamon.

3. In a clean bowl, place the egg whites and lemon
    juice. Whip until the meringue is stiff enough to
    hold in the whisk, but not too stiff. Fold in the

sugar. Blend one third of the meringue into the apple mixture. Then fold in the remainder carefully. Fill the moulds to the brim.

4. Place them onto a tray half filled with water. Bake in a preheated oven at 200°C/400°F/gas mark 6 for 15-20 minutes until well risen. Serve immediately with a scoop of dairy ice cream.

Serves 4

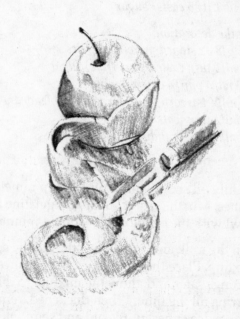

9 CREME AUX CERISES

Cherry brandy cream

Ingredients

For the cream:
50 g/2 oz/¼ cup caster (superfine) sugar
1 small sachet, 10 g/⅓ oz, powdered gelatine
3 egg yolks
300 ml/½ pint/1¼ cups milk
150 ml/¼ pint/⅔ cup whipping cream
3 egg whites, whipped
15 ml/1 tbsp caster sugar

For the decoration:
225 g/8 oz stoned morello cherries
15 ml/1 tbsp caster (superfine) sugar
150 ml/¼ pint/⅔ cup red wine
2.5 ml/½ tsp cornflour (cornstarch) blended with
30 ml/2 tbsp water
45 ml/3 tbsp brandy

Method

1. Lightly oil six 150 ml/¼ pint/⅔ cup ramekin dishes. Mix the caster sugar and gelatine in a metal bowl with the egg yolks. Beat for 4 minutes.

2. Boil the milk and gradually stir into the egg yolk mixture. Place the bowl over a large saucepan of boiling water and allow the mixture to thicken, stirring all the time. When thickened, remove and cool on ice cubes, until cold and semi set.

3. Whip the cream and fold it into the custard. Whip the egg whites to meringue consistency and add the sugar. Fold it into the mixture. Fill the six

prepared moulds to the brim. Chill for 2 hours, then turn out onto six plates.

4. Boil the cherries in the sugar and red wine for 2 minutes. Stir the cornflour and water and add to the cherries. Simmer for 4 minutes. Flavour with brandy and serve with the cherry cream. Serve with macaroons or lighter biscuits (cookies).

Serves 6

CREPES SOUFFLEES AU GRAND MARNIER

Soufflé pancakes

Ingredients

For the pancake mixture:
1 egg
10 ml/2 tsp caster (superfine) sugar
150 ml/¼ pint/⅔ cup milk
50 g/2oz/½ cup flour
Pinch of salt
Oil for cooking

For the orange sauce:
1 orange
45 ml/3 tbsp butter
45 ml/3 tbsp sugar
30 ml/2 tbsp Grand Marnier
2 oranges, segmented

For the soufflé mixture:
2 egg yolks
30 ml/2 tbsp water
45 ml/3 tbsp sugar
4 egg whites
5 ml/1 tsp lemon juice

Method

1. To prepare the pancake batter, combine the egg, sugar, milk, flour and salt in a bowl. Heat 10 ml/ 2 tsp oil in a pancake pan. Pour in 45 ml/3 tbsp of the batter and cook on both sides for 1 minute.

Repeat until you have four pancakes. Cool them on a flat tray. Cut them to 7.5 cm/3 inch diameter rounds.

2.   Grate the rind of the orange. Boil the rind in water for 8 minutes. Drain.

3.   Squeeze the juice from the same orange into a cup. Prepare a syrup in a saucepan with the butter and sugar. When it thickens, add the orange juice and boil for 5 minutes. Add the peel and Grand Marnier.

4.   For the soufflé mixture, mix the egg yolks with the 30 ml/2 tbsp water and 30 ml/2 tbsp of the sugar in a metal bowl. Place the bowl over a saucepan of boiling water. Beat the mixture until it thickens, like a sabayon, three times its volume.

5.   In another bowl, beat the egg whites with the 5ml/1 tsp lemon juice until stiff. Add 15 ml/1 tbsp sugar and beat again. Fold the egg sabayon into the meringue and mix lightly.

6.   Place four flan rings on a baking tray. Line the bottom of each flan ring with a pancake. Fill each with soufflé mixture. Bake in a preheated oven at 200°C/400°F/gas mark 6 for 8-10 minutes. When well risen, carefully remove the rings, cutting the sticking sides with a palette knife. Place each pancake on a plate with a pool of the orange syrup and surround with orange segments.

Serves 4

GATEAU AU FROMAGE FRAIS CITRONE

French lemon cheesecake

Ingredients

225 g/8 oz digestive biscuits (Graham crackers)
100 g/4 oz/½ cup unsalted butter, softened
1 egg, separated

For the filling:
150 g/5 oz/½ cup fromage frais
50 ml/2 fl oz/¼ cup double (heavy) cream
25 g/1 oz/¼ cup flour
65 g/2½ oz/7 tbsp caster (superfine) sugar
Juice and grated rind of 1 lemon

For the decoration:
4 slices of fresh or canned pineapple, cut in small cubes

Method

1.   Oil a 20 cm/8 inch ring tin. Crush the biscuits. Place in a bowl and blend the soft unsalted butter into the crumbs. Add the egg yolk.

2.   Place the mixture in the bottom of the ring and flatten level to a 5 mm/¼ inch thick layer with your knuckles.

3.   In a bowl, blend the fromage frais, cream, 50 g/2 oz/¼ cup of the sugar, flour and lemon juice and grated rind. Beat the egg white until meringue-like, add 15 ml/1 tbsp of sugar and fold into the cheese mixture.

4.   Place the pineapple cubes in the bottom and fill the ring tin with cheese mixture.

5.   Bake in a preheated oven at 200°C/400°F/gas mark 6 for 20-25 minutes. Cool and remove from the tin. Serve with pineapple stewed in syrup flavoured with Kirsch.

Serves 6

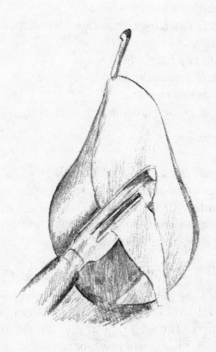

12 TRANCHE AUX NOISETTES

Hazelnut cream slices

This delicious pastry recipe comes from my son Christopher, a master Baker in Southend. We both recommend the basic sweet pastry for all your fruit tarts as one of the very best short sweet pastries.

Ingredients

For the pastry:
100 g/4 oz/½ cup butter, softened
100 g/4 oz/1 cup icing (confectioner's) sugar, sifted
1 egg, beaten
50 g/2 oz/½ cup hazelnuts, ground
250 g/9 oz/2¼ cups soft flour
1.25 ml/¼ tsp salt
2.5 ml/½ tsp ground cinnamon

For the topping:
Jam
100 g/4 oz/½ cup unsalted butter, softened
100 g/4 oz/½ cup caster (superfine) sugar
2 eggs, beaten
75 g/3 oz/¾ cup almond or hazelnuts, ground
25 g/1 oz cake crumbs or breadcrumbs
2 drops of almond, vanilla and lemon essence
250 g/9 oz fresh apricots, about 8, halved and stoned
50 g/2 oz/¼ cup glacé (candied) cherries, 8 in number

For the glaze:
50 g/2 oz/4 tbsp apricot jam, sieved

Method

1.   In a bowl, cream the butter and sugar until fluffy.
         Add the egg and mix in the hazelnuts, flour, salt
         and cinnamon. Blend the pastry without
         overmixing.

2.   On a floured pastry board, roll out the dough to a
         length of 30 cm/12 inches (to fit the baking sheet).
         Cut the pastry into 10 cm/4 inch strips. Line a well
         oiled 30 cm/12 inch baking sheet with the strips.
         Crimp the edges with your thumb and forefinger
         forming a border, or cut 5 mm/¼ inch long strips
         for a border. Brush edges with cold water and
         pinch together. Spread a little jam down the centre.

3.   For the topping, in a bowl cream the butter and
         sugar until light. Add the eggs and blend in the
         ground almonds and cake crumbs. Flavour with
         almond, lemon and vanilla essence. (Use a dropper
         to measure the essences.)

4.   Using a 1 cm/½ inch plain piping tube (tip) filled
         with some of the almond mixture, pipe it onto the
         pastry strips, or use a spoon. Cover the mixture
         with apricot halves in rows. Decorate with halved
         glacé cherries between each apricot.

5.   With any leftover pastry base, thin it down with a
         little cold water to a piping consistency. Using a
         bag fitted with a smaller tube, pipe a zig-zag
         pattern along the top. Bake in a preheated oven at
         190°C/375°F/gas mark 5 for 25 minutes until
         golden brown.

6.   Heat some apricot jam and brush the slices after
         baking while still hot. Serve with cream or custard.

Makes 12 slices

13 BISCUITS AU NOUGAT EN CORNE A LA CREME

Brandy snap cornets

Ingredients

50 g/2 oz/½ cup plain (all purpose) flour
5 ml/1 tsp ground ginger
50 g/2 oz/¼ cup butter or margarine
50 g/2 oz/¼ cup granulated sugar
50 g/2 oz/3 tbsp honey
150 ml/¼ pint/⅔ cup whipped cream

Method

1. Sift the flour and ginger into a bowl.

2. In a saucepan, heat the butter, sugar and honey until dissolved. Add this mixture to the flour, stir well.

3. Arrange teaspoons of the mixture 10 cm/4 inches apart on two greased baking tins, as it will spread on baking. Cook in a preheated oven at 170°C/325°F/gas mark 3 for 8 minutes.

4. Remove the tins from the oven and, after 2 minutes, remove each snap and bend them over a well oiled rolling pin. Remove and slightly shape them into cornets before they cool completely. Work quickly as the snaps become brittle on cooling. Using conical moulds is a better proposition to shape them properly.

5. Fill each cornet with whipped cream just before serving. Serve with sorbet.

Serves 10

Basic sauces and custard creams

 # COULIS DE FRAMBOISES

Raspberry sauce

Ingredients

> 225 g/8 oz/2 cups icing (confectioner's) sugar
> 450 g/1 lb fresh or frozen raspberries
> Juice of 1 lemon
> 10 ml/2 tsp cornflour (cornstarch) blended with
> 30 ml/2 tbsp water

Method

1. For a cold coulis, sprinkle the icing sugar over the raspberries and leave until the juices run. Ad the lemon juice and pass the fruit and syrup through a nylon sieve.

2. For a hot coulis, sieve the ingredients, without the lemon juice, and reheat in a saucepan. Stir the blended cornflour into the boiling purée – cook for 4 minutes. Add the lemon juice.

15 SAUCE AUX ABRICOTS

Apricot glaze

Ingredients

450 g/1 lb apricots, stoned (pitted)
100 g/4 oz/½ cup sugar
Juice of 1 lemon
10 ml/2 tsp cornflour (cornstarch) blended with
45 ml/3 tbsp water

Method

1. For a cold coulis, liquidize the mixture to a thin purée, then boil for 4 minutes. Cool.

2. For a hot coulis, boil the same mixture and add the blended cornflour. Boil for 4 minutes more.

16 CERISES JUBILEE

Black cherry Jubilee

Ingredients

450 g/1 lb black cherries, stoned (pitted)
250 ml/8 fl oz/1 cup red wine
225 g/8 oz/1 cup sugar
2.5 ml/½ tsp ground cinnamon
5 ml/1 tsp cornflour (cornstarch) blended with
45 ml/3 tbsp water
45 ml/3 tbsp Kirsch or brandy

Method

1. Boil the cherries in the wine with the sugar for 5 minutes. Add the cinnamon.

2. Add the blended cornflour to the cherries. Cook for 4 minutes to clear the starch. Lastly stir in the Kirsch.

17 CREME ANGLAISE

English egg custard

Ingredients

> 6 egg yolks
> 75 g/3 oz/6 tbsp caster (superfine) sugar
> 600 ml/1 pint/2½ cups milk
> 1 vanilla pod (bean)
> 25 g/1 oz/2 tbsp unsalted butter or 45 ml/3 tbsp double (heavy) cream

Method

1. In a stainless steel bowl, beat the egg yolks and sugar for 5 minutes.

2. Boil the milk with the vanilla pod. Gradually pour it over the egg mixture, stirring, removing the vanilla pod. Place the bowl over a saucepan of boiling water and keep on whisking until the custard thickens and coats the back of a spoon. Remove from the heat and blend in the butter or cream.

   Variation: This custard can be flavoured with brandy, rum or Grand Marnier.

18 | CREME PATISSIERE

Confectioner's custard

Ingredients

600 ml/1 pint/2½ cups milk
1 vanilla pod (bean)
2 egg yolks
75 g/3 oz/6 tbsp caster (superfine) sugar
25 g/1 oz/¼ cup strong bread flour
15 g/½ oz/1 tbsp cornflour (cornstarch)
15 ml/1 tbsp icing (confectioner's) sugar

Method

1. In a large heavy based pan, boil the milk with the vanilla pod.

2. In a bowl, whisk the egg yolks and sugar, then add the flour and cornflour. Pour half of the milk into this mixture, stirring, and whisk well. Reheat in a saucepan until it begins to boil, then stir in the remaining milk, removing the vanilla pod. Simmer for 4 minutes.

3. Sprinkle the icing sugar over the cream to prevent a skin forming, or use some melted unsalted butter.

19 GANACHE DE CHOCOLAT AU RHUM

Chocolate cream

Ingredients

> *150 ml/¼ pint/⅔ cup double (heavy) cream*
> *100 g/4 oz/⅔ cup dark chocolate, grated or chopped*
> *30 ml/2 tbsp dark rum (optional)*

Method

1. Bring the cream just to the boil and add the grated chocolate. Stir well to obtain a smooth mixture.

2. Remove from the heat and add the rum. Store in a bowl in a cold place until required. Use to flavour sauces.

20 CREME DE SABAYON

Wine custard

Ingredients

1 egg
3 egg yolks
50 g/2 oz/¼ cup caster (superfine) sugar
225 ml/8 fl oz/1 cup dry sherry

Method

1. In a stainless steel bowl, whisk the egg, yolks and sugar for 4 minutes.

2. Place the bowl over a saucepan of boiling water. Using a balloon whisk, beat the mixture, gradually adding the sherry. Cook until the texture of whipped cream. Serve either warm or cold.

21 SORBET AU CHARENTAIS MELON

Melon sorbet

Ingredients

1 medium ripe melon
Juice of 1 lemon
100 g/4 oz/½ cup caster (superfine) sugar
25 g/1 oz/¼ cup icing (confectioner's) sugar
15 g/½ oz powdered gelatine
30 ml/2 tbsp cream

Method

1. Split the melon and remove the seeds. Measure 225 g/8 oz melon pulp and juices.

2. Boil the melon pulp and juice with the sugars for 2 minutes. Dissolve the gelatine in a little water in a bowl over a pan of hot water. Add to the melon.

3. Cool and place in trays lined with greaseproof (wax) paper. Freeze for 2 hours. Unmould and whisk with the cream in a bowl. Refreeze.

Index – ENGLISH